D0061790

Preface

Servant friends have surrounded and supported me while writing this book. My debt is immense:

To the real Fred of chapter 1 for his example of alertness to and compassion for the needs of another person.

To Dan Siemasko for sharing himself in chapter 2, for writing chapters 5 and 9.

To Charlie LaVallee, Shadyside Presbyterian Church, Pittsburgh, who lives out the concept of "tough love" about which he teaches in his Relationship Seminars. The better ideas of chapter 10 are his.

To Harvey Beach for ideas and encouragement about the topic of forgiving.

To Rachel Walters who developed the discussion questions, but more importantly makes life worthwhile as my best friend.

Deep appreciation and admiration are expressed for Gary Konow who at one point was to have been co-author. Due to physical problems (from which he has, through the Lord's mercy, recovered) it was not possible for him to do that. His considerable professional expertise, life experience and spiritual insight are worthy of a book, which I hope he will write.

Thank you: Helen Brinks for your typing skills; Pine Rest Christian Hospital for the opportunity to present workshops on these topics as part of its commitment to help people live in wholeness; and Regal Books, especially Senior Editor Don Pugh, for interest in the manuscript and patience with its author.

Many incidents are, in essential dynamics, based on actual events. Information about persons, though, has been scrambled and revised so that no actual person can be identified from the information in this book. Any similarity to real persons, living or dead, results only from the fact that in so many ways we are all alike, which fact gives us the possibility of being servant friends.

This book covers some of the topics included in the author's *Amity: Friendship in Action,* a training manual for use in skill-building workshops; information is available from Christian Helpers, Inc., 5500 Waterbury Pl. S.E., Kentwood, MI 49508.

"May the God of peace . . . equip you with everything good for doing his will, and may he work in us what is pleasing to him, through Jesus Christ, to whom be glory for ever and ever. Amen" (Heb. 13:20,21).

Chapter One

Four Guys: Two to Die

Who decides who dies? You do. I do. Don't be so quick to say it isn't so. When two lives merge into the same experience, both persons change—always a little, often a lot. Sometimes an eternity's worth.

Paths cross. Every day we are part of other persons' lives. Our actions always affect them—to help them live more fully or to cause them to die a little. We make an impact and the results add up. When paths cross, eternity is at stake.

I want to tell you a couple of stories to illustrate these ideas. The events in these stories might someday happen to you, or maybe they have happened to you already and you didn't even know it. The stories are both about two men, ordinary guys in most respects. It doesn't matter that the persons and the places are disguised to protect those who could yet be hurt by the truth; the stories are true, tombstone true.

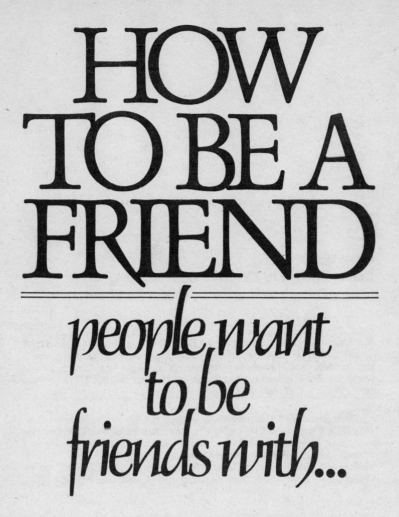

HOW TO BE A FRIEND

people want to be friends with...

RICHARD P. WALTERS

Regal Books
Division of G/L Publications
Ventura, CA U.S.A.

Other good reading:
Caring Enough to Confront by David Augsburger
Caring Enough to Forgive by David Augsburger

The foreign language publishing of all Regal Books is under the direction of GLINT. GLINT provides financial and technical help for the adaptation, translation and publishing of books in more than 85 languages for millions of people worldwide. For information regarding translation, contact: GLINT, P.O. Box 6688, Ventura, California 93006.

For the sake of easier reading, the use of the pronouns *he, him*, and *his* in this publication refers for the most part to both male and female in the generic sense.

Published by Regal Books
A Division of GL Publications
Ventura, California 93006
Printed in U.S.A.

Library of Congress Catalog Card No. 81-52163
ISBN 0-8307-0746-8

To my parents,
for living the principles
of servant friendship.

Contents

Killing Rats

It could have happened yesterday, I remember it that well; but I know it has been a long time because it happened in a hot, dry, dusty place where I haven't lived for many years.

The D & L Truck Stop in that small town was a heavy-duty place where long-haul rigs would wheel in off the arrow-straight prairie roads to refuel. The D & L was a big stone building with a cafe, three bays for service, a forest of pumps and an acre of sharp chunky gravel. It was an oasis, a break in bleak and roaring monotony, an event.

Big trucks would come thundering in, backfire belching out of straight exhausts as they growled to a stop, air brakes hissing defiantly. The drivers of those rigs would dismount and swagger into the cafe to coffee up, wolf down a pit-stop porterhouse, tell lies and tease waitresses, and maybe buy a fresh pack of smokes or a sweet-scented blotter-paper girlie to hang on the dash. In the time it took to have three cups of coffee with nine Hank Williams songs the trucks would be gassed up, the bugs scoured off the windshield. Then it was back down the road— a crunch of gravel and cloud of dust, truck and driver snorting and bellowing in unison, heading out onto the sticky blacktop into the heat waves ahead.

The key person around the D & L was Burke Dressen, owner and general ramrod, the guy who made it all happen. Even back then Burke's leathery face looked a hundred years old but his coal black hair looked 20 and he'd fight any man who asked him if he dyed it. If he fought, he won. Always. Amazing, for a little man. People wondered where the power came from. Some people even speculated that there was some mysterious, horrible wound in his past that fired the hammer-fisted rage on those rare occasions when Burke fought. But the speculation was quiet, because you just didn't mess with Burke Dressen.

Of course he was busy most of the time anyway. And happy. Who wouldn't be, raking in money like that? Sitting on a gold mine, people said, and I guess they were right. The trucks rolled in and the money rolled in and there wasn't a man around who didn't know the place and wish he owned a piece of the cash register. Those were the glory days of the D & L Truck Stop.

But glory is fleeting. Everything changes and when things changed at the D & L they got really bad. Burke remembers how it was when things got bad. He can tell it better than I can, so I'll let him speak for himself. Burke?

Well, I been in the service station business for, oh, as long as I can remember. Started out greasing T-model Fords way back when and worked my way up to finally gittin' my own place here. It don't look like nothin' now but we had some kind of a place if you'd a seen it in its day—10, 12 years ago. Open 24 hours and busy all the time.

Then they opened up the bypass and of course that dried up the traffic through town just like it was s'posed to. Even more. So pretty soon I had to lay off a couple of my men and then the restaurant got slow and I had to close that and that took the whole thing down another notch right with it.

Pretty soon it was just me and the gas pumps. Well, you can't do no repairs havin' to run the pumps too, and I couldn't get no decent help that would stay with me. They all wanted to get paid like they was brain surgeons or somethin'.

So there it was for a long time. And meantime, my ol' lady, she got fed up and she moved out on me—that's while my boy Jim was in the army. So I got me a little trailer and put it down at the end of the street near my friend Jess's house.

Things just went on like that. Me and the pumps and cars, oh fairly steady enough but, shoot, you can't sell no amount of gas just fillin' cars with them dinky little tanks. I was gettin' by, though, even if I did have some big payments on the place. But my livin' expenses in the little trailer was low enough, that's for sure.

All that was okay as far as it went, which wasn't very far. Once in a while one of the old boys would drive in off the bypass to see how things was but you could see it made them pretty uncomfortable seeing that things was so different and I don't think none of 'em ever come back the second time. I didn't blame 'em, but I wished they had.

Jim came back and he got married and she got pregnant and I got older and got a grandchild and things went on. And nothin' seemed to change very much 'cept maybe the days got longer and the summers were hotter and the winters colder and the trailer, well, it was gettin' awful small.

Jess died and that was awful rough on me. The old lady didn't care if she got any money offa me, and that helped a little, but it woulda been nice to have somebody to spend it on, what little I had.

Of course, there was Jim and his family; they was good to me in their own way. Jim, he'd picked up a drinkin' habit somethin' awful in the service and it got worse 'n worse. I hated to see that. His wife, she didn't care; fact was, she liked him stone cold drunk so she could run anywhere she pleased. I knew what was going on and she knew I knew it and she didn't even care. That hurt awful bad 'cause they had two kids when that was going on and I could see what was happenin' to Jim and to the kids, too. I didn't care about her. And his drinkin' started costin' me a lot a money—fixin' up his messes, you see.

Jim was my only child. I always thought he might go in business with me but I didn't have even a two-man business and, well, he was a no-account kind of worker I wouldn't want anyway, much as I hate to say it. I'd fired a lotta guys who was a whole lot better men than Jim. It hurt to think about that.

This is the way it was, year after year, for a long time. Sometimes I'd think back and wonder how I coulda let things go wrong and try to think how to get things goin' happy again, and it got awful discouragin'. What with the ol' lady gone, and Jess gone, and Jim all messed up, and now this pain in my back comin' on, things really got heavy on my mind. The time just drug by. Business was slow and I just sat there watchin' the tools get rusty and thinkin' about how things was and gettin' more and more discouraged.

One day it really got bad. The worst it ever was up to then. I don't know why, 'cause it started out okay that day. A guy came in. Had four tires he'd got somewheres he wanted mounted. This was about eight in the mornin'. Said could he get the car back at five. "Sure," I said, thinkin' I'd do it in the afternoon when I felt better. Well, that was the day it seemed like ever'thing busted loose in my head. Like, ever'thing that could go wrong did. I cracked up like I'd been hit by a train, and it woulda been okay if I had been. Maybe better.

I just got to thinkin' about how things had been and how things could be and how things never was going to be like they oughta be and then I just cut loose cryin' like a baby with the colic and I just cried and cried. Well, I couldn't stop and for once I was glad there wasn't no business. I don't know how long that went on but it musta been a long time. Then I didn't feel like doin' no work so I went back in the shop. It was nice and dark in there, and dirty but that didn't matter. I was used to that. I pulled an old wooden box into the corner and just sat and sat and sat.

A lot of time went by and some people musta come and left. In the afternoon I got to thinkin' how it would look for someone to see me, so I ran out and got the "open" sign and brought it in. I just got in when someone drove up but I ducked under the old desk we had up front. I just crouched down there. Hey, it felt pretty good 'cept I woulda felt pretty stupid if anyone'd seen me then. I heard the engine turn off and they honked but pretty soon the engine started again and he drove off, or she did. Prob'ly a man though, scratched off real fast like a man. Or some smart-alecky kid. Smart-aleck kids and their fancy cars; I didn't even like to sell gas to 'em.

I got mad and I cried and my neck felt like it was bustin' off and I just wanted to take a axe to it. I crawled off to the back room. I couldn't stand up and walk back cause somebody mighta seen me. I felt pretty stupid again, but my back hurt like somethin' anyway so standin' up wouldn'ta been so easy anyhow. I went back to the box in the corner and sat some more. Then I thought about the tires but I just couldn't stand the thought of doin' that so I just kept on sittin', waitin' for somethin' to happen. Just sittin' and cryin' some and sittin' and sittin'.

Well, finally I heard someone come in and as soon as I heard him I knowed it must be that guy with the tires. I figured I was in trouble cause his car was still sittin' there where he left it. I thought maybe if I was quiet he wouldn't find me back there in the dark. I didn't want no trouble so I just sat there—real quiet. Of course, he looked all around and he said "Hello" but I stayed quiet. I didn't want to talk, to work, or to do *nothin'*. *Just leave me alone, that's all.* That's what I was thinkin'. Finally, he come in the back and he walked all around and then he seen me and walked over. I never even looked up. I just sat there starin' at the floor, and then at his shoes when he finally moved in on me. But he couldn't take a hint. He couldn't see I wanted to be left alone. He couldn't see how much I hurt. So he says, nice and polite, "It doesn't look like you've even started on my car. I thought you were going to have it done by five."

I just stared at them fancy shiny shoes and the ends of his slick suit pants and I thought, *I'll bet that guy couldn't change his own tires if his life depended on it and he had all the tools in this shop and all the time in the world!* But I didn't say nothin'.

Then he says, gettin' a little uppity, "Well, this morning you said you would do it and you had all day."

I didn't say nothin'.

"Are you going to do it or aren't you?"

Now he was gettin' mad, that was easy to tell. I didn't want no fight. Not then. So I said, "I'll do it."

"When?"

I was gettin' mad myself then, thinkin' about why couldn't he leave me alone but I was too tired and I hurt too bad to get mad so I just said, "Now."

"Okay. Then I'll walk home for supper and I'll be back at seven to pick it up. Is that okay?"

"Okay."

He stomped off then, finally. Oh, I guess he was a nice enough fella; he was okay when he came back at seven. But, it wasn't my day.

That day was the one that really got me thinkin' about the future—stuff like that. Did an awful lot of thinkin'. Didn't sleep much, just sat around and thought. It seemed like a long, long time.

The rest of Burke's story was in the paper. Maybe you saw it:

Service Station Operator Dies

Burke Dressen, age 57, died late Monday
night from a gunshot wound. The body

was discovered by his son late this morning. According to the coroner's report, Dressen apparently put the end of a small bore shotgun in his mouth and . . .

Pushing Pills

The second story concerns a fellow named Randy Jonas. Let's just let him tell his own story.

I'm a registered pharmacist. You could probably call me a pill pusher and maybe that's all it seems like to you but it takes a lot of training and it's complicated work. I graduated from our state university school of pharmacy three years ago and studied hard to get through.

Ginger and I got married two years ago. We'd been planning that for a long time. I'm 25, she's 23, and we don't have any kids.

People say we were made for each other, that we are the all-American young married couple, and stuff like that. I don't know. Ginger, yes. Hey, she's beautiful! And me? Okay, my image isn't too bad, either—six feet tall, 180 pounds, naturally curly hair and perfect teeth and all that stuff—but, let me tell you, there have been lots of times I've looked in the mirror and didn't see a thing that looked good to me. Nothing. I didn't want to. I didn't even want to exist!

For most people going into a drugstore is an easy thing. Their biggest worry may be how much the prescription will cost or how long they may have to wait.

For me working there, it got to be so I couldn't stand to go inside. I dreaded it—just flat out hated it. It was like going into a mausoleum. All those little drawers at the pharmacy seemed to be full of death. It was as though some big door would slam shut and the lights would go out and I'd be trapped in there forever.

This went on for a long time and it was really weird and scary. When I started to realize how weird it was, that scared me all the more.

At home I was uptight all the time, and it got so Ginger and I were fighting. We used to think that would never happen. Then I started sleeping on the hide-a-bed and things just went from bad to worse.

One day I was going to work and the closer I got to the store the worse I felt. My hands sweat so I could hardly hold the steering wheel. I began to think, *Why should I even go to that stupid place if I hate it so much?* So I decided not to go and just gunned the car and roared on past. I yelled, "Shove it!" as I drove by and then I laughed and laughed and just about ran off the road. That made me laugh too. I noticed a lot of tears with the laughing and that scared me again and I got sad and worried. I didn't know what was happening to me or what to do about it but I knew for sure I wasn't going to the store that day.

I got a bottle of wine and drove out to a park. Hunching down low behind the wheel, I watched the lake and sipped my wine and just generally mellowed out. It was the best I'd felt in a long time but it wasn't very good. I was there a long time, just thinking and sipping and thinking. A guy came over and stood by the car. We talked for a while but I could see he wasn't my type. I drove off to get a hamburger and some more wine and went to another park. When it finally came quitting time at the store, I drove home.

I almost lost my job over that. I gave the boss a big snow job that he didn't believe but he couldn't prove different. Ginger threatened to leave me, so I knew I had to shape up and I wanted to but I didn't know how.

After that I made sure I at least got to the store and stood up there and did my thing of counting out pills, typing up the forms and labels, keeping the records (what a drag that was), and explaining things to people. I was surviving and, even though the boss was pretty surly, he began to get over it.

Sometimes I'd get this weird urge that if there was a big pile of pills, say six feet high, I'd just dive into them and crawl down to the bottom of the pile and never come up. I could see myself down there, like I had x-ray vision. There I was curled up like a sleeping baby with a warm blanket of all those pills and it didn't look too bad at all. It looked pretty good, really.

Things weren't going too good at home either. Ginger and I had quit talking, except she kept saying, "Let's have a baby." Good grief! That's the last thing I needed—more responsibility. Then I got the idea she was running around, and I didn't like thinking that, but I did and I thought about it an awful lot.

It went on like this for about a year. Some days were real bad, some not so bad, but never any days that you would call real good.

I could see things weren't getting better. I was sure they never would. Maybe for someone else, but not for me. I didn't like it the way it was but I didn't know what I could do about it. Oh, I knew I ought to go see a shrink or something, but I couldn't do that.

I'd think about doing myself in. I'd think about that a lot. Didn't really think I would, but it was easy to see how people could. And it was a possibility. It would be easy.

One time I was working nights and I was running the whole store alone. It didn't happen very often but I didn't much care; in a way I kind of liked it because it kept me busy.

Anyway, there I was when this guy came in. He was about my age, dark red hair, wearing a dark blue baseball jacket. He had a prescription which I took and he stood around while I filled it and neither of us said anything. So I gave him the meds and he paid and then a funny thing happened.

He said, kind of matter-of-fact but I thought he really meant it, "You know, it must be pretty complicated to run a place like this with so much different stuff to keep track of."

Well that's for sure, so I said, "Yeah. It's a pain in the neck sometimes. With the pills especially. You've got to account for every last one of them."

"Wow!" he said. "That'd get kind of tedious!"

"Yeah! And for what?" I kind of blurted that out, louder than I meant to.

"Sounds like you're getting pretty tired of it. Things must be rough here . . ."

I butted right in. I couldn't help it. "Yeah! Rough here, rough at home, and rough everywhere as far as I'm concerned." I could feel tears filling my eyes and I didn't even care. "But it doesn't have to be that way forever." I didn't want to say that, and I knew what was coming next and I for sure didn't want to talk about that, but I knew I was going to. In a way I did want to talk about it. "I could change things quick and painless. Being a pharmacist, it would be easy. I've got everything I need right here."

"That's a pretty big decision. Things must seem pretty hopeless if you're thinking along those lines."

"I can't do anything right to please anybody. The boss is down on me, my wife is down on me, and I'm down on me!" My stomach churned as I spat the words out, like the words themselves were poisonous, even though I knew it wasn't the boss or Ginger that needed to change, it was me.

The stranger stood there motionless, leaning slightly toward me over the white Formica counter. His manner spoke a friendly, quiet confidence and it seemed to me that he understood what was happening to me and cared unselfishly about it. I remember that I wondered why he would care, why this guy, an ordinary guy walking in off the street, should take such an uncommon interest in my confusion and fear and anger and still be unselfish about it. But it didn't matter that I didn't know why.

"From what you say then, you're feeling pretty worthless and kind of trapped—like you can't stand the way things are now, yet you can't imagine how they could get better."

"That's it!"

"I think things *can* get better for you. It seems pretty early to give up. Incidentally, my name's Fred."

"Mine's Randy." And we shook hands.

"You play tennis, Randy?"

"Sure. Well, for exercise. I'm no competitor."

"That's my style. I wish we could get together sometime."

"Yeah. That'd be okay."

"Look, Randy, I don't want to be barging into your life, but it seems like you've got a heavy mood laying on you and, well, if there's any way I can help you with that, I'd like a chance to try. That's all—no tricks up my sleeve."

"Yeah. Good."

"I'm off work tomorrow. Any chance for that tennis?"

So that's how it went. We played tennis several times and then Fred and his wife invited us over to their place and along the way I began to see that maybe things could get better and finally, with Fred's encouragement, I took the big step of going to a professional counselor. There was a long process of sorting things out, learning new things, breaking old habits and building things back better than they ever had been. That wasn't easy but it was worth every bit of effort.

Looking back I see what a fragile thread my life hung on that day Fred came in. And how amazing it was that he could notice that I was up over my head in feeling lousy, that I was within an inch of total despair. No one else ever noticed, or if they did, they didn't care enough to say anything! Well, a lot of people don't want to be nosey and there's something to be said for that, but Fred wasn't nosey. He cared.

Fred cared enough to try to understand—to talk about it and let me talk—and that made all the difference to me. And to Ginger. And to our son. He's going to be born next month!

There they are, two stories about paths that crossed, lives that intermingled. Burke and Randy were two ordinary guys in extraordinary distress. One's path was crossed by a Christian, the other's by a non-believer. I know that's the way it was because I was the man with the tires, blind to Burke's profound suffering, so immersed in my own trivial needs as to not see his gigantic needs. That was me, the Christian.

Did my insensitivity cause Burke to shoot himself? No. The seeds of that decision were planted decades before I met him and nurtured through countless errors and sins that only he could have known. If I had seen his distress, could my response have made a difference? Perhaps, perhaps not. I don't know. But I do know that my attitude showed no acceptance and my conversation offered no hope. My self-centeredness may not have hurt him but it has hurt me, and I wish things had been different.

Several years later my path crossed with Fred's. My life was enriched by our friendship as I saw Fred's concern for broken people, his unreserved acceptance of them as worthwhile beings, his accurate discernment of their distress, and his unselfish attending to their needs. It was just as he had done with Randy. It was bewildering at first because his compassion went beyond what was supposed to be possible apart from Christ, and Fred did not identify himself as a Christian. I often felt ashamed as I saw the Christlikeness of Fred's behavior in contrast to my own behavior which fell so short of biblical ideals. That contrast unsettles me still, as it ought.

What about you? Does your life ever influence another person in an important way? Should it? Are you ready to be used fully as God's servant to others? Or are you more concerned about your tires?

Discussion Questions

1. In what way do we have a part in deciding who dies, and when they die?
2. List the succession of events that led to Burke's depression. How did they affect his life?
3. How might the story of Burke have had a different ending?
4. By society's standards, Randy Jonas had a good job and a number of pluses in his life. How do you account for his attitude?
5. What descriptive words can you use to portray Fred's interaction with Randy? What was the key element that made this different from the story about Burke?
6. Give examples from your own experience when you exercised servant friendship—or when you wished you had after the opportunity slipped by.
7. How can you be more alert to opportunities for servant friendship?
8. What populations of persons in your community need servant friends?

Chapter Two

Servant Friendship: Love in Action

Pain exists. You know that from personal experience, and you know that there are people in whose life pain is far greater than yours.

Fear, sorrow, loneliness, rage and despair are all around us; maybe we notice, maybe we don't. A servant friend notices and wants to do something about it.

Servant friends care—deeply, unselfishly, patiently. And they put the caring into action.

What do they do? Servant friends—

—add more to other persons' lives than they take away

—affirm, knowing that building up another's self-esteem does not diminish their own

—share themselves, including their flaws so others may learn from their mistakes

—give trust, and deserve trust

—discern, recognizing the difference between cold facts and a snow job

—do not insist on equality, being willing to inconvenience themselves for the convenience of others

—invite others to come out from behind their walls of defense

—willingly pay the cost of friendship, even the high cost of abandoning self-centeredness

—love you because you *are*, not because you have or are going to

—take the initiative to help

—represent our Lord. A servant friend is love in action.

Servant friendship is a calling to follow the example of Jesus Christ, the perfect Servant Friend. For us, servant friendship as described above is unattainable. But we are responsible in the Spirit of Christ and with the help of our Father to do the best we can.

It means going beyond the take-it-or-leave-it level of acquaintance. Compare the two lists below.

Acquaintance	**Friendship**
Relationship	*Relationship*
limited to:	*based on:*
knowing about	knowing
my convenience	unselfishness
indifference	caring
independence	interdependence
isolation	involvement
taking	giving
my good	our good

We all need at least one servant friend. The best way to get one is to be one. May I be your servant friend?

This is a book about servant friendship. This is the chapter that lays down the assumptions and principles. It's the most important chapter and, yes, it's probably the least interesting. It sure is hard to write! But if we don't build on truth we're doomed. Consider figure 1. Don't try to construct this object in three dimensions! It's impossible, because the plan is not built on truth.

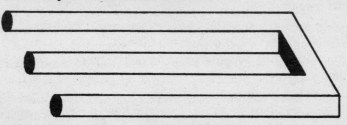

Figure 1

There are many books these days that promise to teach you foolproof techniques for making friends, helping or influencing people, and for settling conflict. Some of the suggestions these books make are excellent; but many of their plans are no more reliable than the diagram in figure 1 because they are based on the world's assumptions rather than God's truth. So, let's state some principles.

We must take into account man's fallen nature. Man is not, as most secular humanists believe, inherently good. Man's evil nature affects how people respond to the good that we do and, as the apostle Paul pointed out, also affects our own performance: "I do not understand what I do. For what I want to do I do not do, but what I hate I do. . . . As it is, it is no longer I myself who do it, but it is sin living in me" (Rom. 7:15,17).

Often we know what to do but we fail to do it. We need God's help. The more we seek God's partnership in our activities, the more effective we will be in servant friendship.

A prevalent error is to assume that people are objects which can, with the proper skills, be manipulated in much the same way that a car can be manipulated once the driver has learned the proper driving skills. Not so. While we can learn the *probable* effects of our actions on others, the God-given freedom of spirit that each person has leaves them with control over their responses to us.

Skills are important; motives are even more important. The servant friend who loves God with all his heart, soul, and mind (see Matt. 22:37) and therefore loves others even as Christ loves him (see John 15:12) strives to glorify God, not self. This person may become an effective servant friend without formal training in friendship skills while a selfish Christian may learn all the skills in the world and still be ineffective as a friend. If we only wear the mask of a servant friend we will be seen as phony to those we try to help and our efforts will blow up in our faces.

God's leadership in how friendship develops and in guiding what we say and do is more important than anything else. This book will give you knowledge about friendship methods, but that is meaningless without wisdom to apply it in authentic and unselfish love. God is our source of wisdom and love.

• Unselfish compassion is not the exclusive property of the Christian; the natural human spirit has within it great capacity for caring. We saw that in Fred's compassionate response to Randy. Conversion does not guarantee compassion; it doesn't even guarantee courtesy. We saw that in Rich's blindness to Burke's needs.

• Recognizing distress and responding to it are skills of service. They rise out of a foundation of love. The foundation is commanded of Christians; its expression in service is imperative if our generation is to know Christ.

• Our sinful nature leads us toward preoccupation with self. With maturity in Christian living we become less preoccupied with self so that with thanksgiving for God's grace through Christ we can be led by the Holy Spirit to "carry each other's burdens" (Gal. 6:2).

• People get tightly embedded in dismal life-styles.

They change gradually. Dan Siemasko describes, in summary, his own "expiration and renewal."

Ignorance and apathy: I don't know and I don't care! Besides, even if I sensed how badly I hurt, why would it matter? No one else cares, so why change?

On guard and pretentious: I'm safe, protected in the prison of my facades. As long as I don't move, I can keep all my junk covered.

Self-suspicion and fear: I'm a yellow phony, afraid to be found out. Risk ridicule and rejection? No thank you!

Hopelessness and despair: All's been done; there's nothing I can add. Things are out of my hands; I'll take what comes and try to adapt to it.

Out of touch and angry: Leave me alone!

And, finally, words of change—

Pain and crying: Suffering has forced me into a corner, into surrender, "Help! . . . Anybody, help!"

Openness and acceptance: Someone has made room for me to express myself. Ver-r-ry carefully I'll unveil my psyche and streak a bit of me.

Trust and caring: Through the intimacy and affirmation of others I have a place to explore. I'll begin trusting me and begin to find my identity, my uniqueness, and my value.

Risk and commitment: I could start to face reality, to evaluate life's questions, to be challenged, to make decisions, to commit myself, and to get going.

Focus and autonomy: Through gathering in and sorting out, defining and outlining, asserting and proclaiming, I could penetrate the confusion. I feel free to act on my own.

Belief and decision: I am convinced of the power of Jesus. Now I can shed the old and become new. Death is ended, birth pangs endured; life begins, thank God!

Meaning and faith: The new man, me, has purpose: to serve Christ and person. With the companionship of the Holy Spirit and friends, I am no longer alone. With strength from God and friends I don't have to act just on my own. We live!

Servant friendship begins at the point of the other person's need; looks ahead in realistic hope; and moves at a pace that is right, slow enough to be tolerable but fast enough to nurture optimism. Its direction is toward God; its purpose is renewal.

What effect might we have as servant friend? Dan Siemasko again writes of the meaning of friendship in his personal experience, with "your" referring to the collective friendship of a group of believers known as the Pittsburgh Experiment.

> *I meet the world: my story*
> Their authority, my submission;
> > Their hypocrisy, my criticism;
> Their judgments, my defensiveness;
> > Our distance, our non-growth.
> My withering, their indifference;
> > My aloneness, their separateness.

> *I meet the God people: our story*
> My cry, your presence;
> > My distrust, your invitation;
> My shame, your spontaneity;
> > My hiding, your freedom.
> My experimenting, your prayers;
> > My doubts, your challenge;
> My funny feelings, your listening;
> > My self-hate; your love.
> My stepping out, your encouragement;
> > My choice, your applause;

My anxiety, your understanding;
   Our togetherness, our growing.
My hopes, your confirmation;
   My faith, ours—and we have only just begun.

• Servant friendship is founded on unconditional love. Unconditional means meeting people (1) to know them (2) to love them (3) to serve them; to seek *their* best interests. If I profess unconditional love to others, the only qualification they need in order to receive my love is that they exist. That's all!

It does not mean meeting people to persuade them, to change them, to use them. If I explained the plan of salvation to someone and he ridiculed me, and I loved him less—it wasn't unconditional.

Have you loved unconditionally? Probably you have, at moments at least, but never out of your own resources. Your humanness can't go further than half way. You can't love others unconditionally until you love God unconditionally. When you do, the power of the Holy Spirit cuts the strings between your selfishness and the other person, and the second half of the conditions fall away.

The power to love unconditionally is freely available. We think it's rare because we seek it incorrectly. Seek God; the other follows.

• Servant friendship is the expression of love and therefore the obligation of every Christian. Jesus said, "This is my command: Love each other" (John 15:17). He expressed His love to persons in many ways.

He commands that our love, too, be expressed: "I chose you to go and bear fruit—fruit that will last" (John 15:16). There are several ways in which we are to express love to others: to encourage, please our neighbors, bear the infirmities of the weak, confront, warn, see to it that good teaching is provided, share and show hospitality.[1]

These are apart from corporate responsibilities of a group of believers which might be assigned to office bearers; these are responsibilities of all believers.

Jesus has not left us with an assignment and no way to carry it out. He promises that "the Father will give you whatever you ask in my name" (John 15:16). Success is not contingent upon our ability, but upon devotion and obedience.

• Through training, caring Christians can learn to recognize and respond effectively to persons wounded by our broken world. In chapters 3-5 we talk about part of that training.

First we'll consider possible applications of servant friendship and read in chapter 3 an account of effective friendship. Chapter 4 describes common barriers to friendship, and a narrative in chapter 5 contrasts selfish caring with true friendship.

The rest of the book presents skills that are important if you want to H-E-L-P. We'll divide the process of giving help into four phases: Hello, Exploration, Learning, Progress.

The *Hello* phase is strategic because if we don't meet, if we don't make at least a minimal connection, I can't help you. Chapter 6 covers some basic, but very important, relational doors through which we enter for servant friendship.

The *Exploration* phase involves understanding each other. Chapters 7 and 8 deal with listening and trust, two essential elements in gaining mutual understanding.

The *Learning* phase may involve me, as a servant friend, in sharing my own attitudes and experiences, and even in pointing out to you areas in your life in which you need to improve. Chapters 9 and 10 cover self-disclosure and confrontation.

The *Progress* phase moves toward closure for problems. It is not enough to get acquainted and explore our dreams and frustrations; we must resolve the conflicts or inadequacies that keep us from fully meaningful living. Chapters 11 through 13 teach about apologizing, forgiving, and decision-making.

The story in the next chapter is about servant friendship. It illustrates many of these principles.

• There are no limits to our potential for service to others if we allow God to work through us. The potential is as limitless as God's mercy, as limitless as His immeasurable power, as limitless as His relentless love.

• As we follow the Holy Spirit's leadership toward total involvement in life, we are likely to be led into activities of servanthood that stretch our courage, extend our patience, and force us to step aside and allow God to work through us instead of in spite of us.

He may give us opportunities for service that seem much more difficult than we can handle, but there is *nothing* that we cannot accomplish if God wants us to and we allow Him to be part of the process. God never asks of us more than we can do. "For God is at work within you, helping you want to obey him, and then helping you do what he wants" (Phil. 2:13, *TLB*).

He will help us learn to be patient, as Paul learned to be patient (see 2 Tim. 3:10,11).

He has given us His Word as the most important element in our being equipped for servant friendship: "All Scripture is God-breathed and is useful for teaching, rebuking, correcting and training in righteousness, so that the man of God may be thoroughly equipped for *every* good work" (2 Tim. 3:16,17).

We can develop in the personal qualities of love, joy, peace, patience, kindness, goodness, faithfulness, gentleness and self-control (see Gal. 5:22,23). And when we run out of any of these we can ask for what we need, knowing that we will receive, for Jesus said, "My Father will give you whatever you ask in my name" (John 16:23).

Why do we have these privileges? Because God loves us, and that love makes it possible for us to be courageous in our servanthood. "If God is for us, who can be against us? He who did not spare his own Son, but gave him up for us all—how will he not also, along with him, graciously give us all things?" (Rom. 8:31,32).

What does servant friendship look like in practice? Different than in theory because of the human blunder element. But, as you read the story in the next chapter you will see that in spite of mistakes, or perhaps because of a willingness to take responsibility for them, servant friendship can be a powerful force.

Discussion Questions

1. Give some examples from Christ's life which illustrate His servant friendship. Discuss these in light of the characteristics listed at the beginning of this chapter.
2. Where is the error in the belief that people are objects which can be manipulated "in much the same way that a car can be manipulated once the driver has learned the proper driving skills"?
3. Discuss the statement, "Conversion does not guarantee compassion; it doesn't even guarantee courtesy." Do you agree or disagree?
4. What does "conditional love" mean to you? Include in your answer some of the things it does not mean.
5. Refer to the Scriptures cited near the end of this chapter (from Philippians, Timothy, Galatians, John, and Romans) and relate what they mean specifically to you.

Note

1. See verses such as Romans 15:1,2; Colossians 3:16; 2 Timothy 2:2; Hebrews 10:25; 13:1,2,16; James 5:19,20.

Chapter Three

The Power
of Friendship

Sterling wore a carnation in his lapel every day of the year. It was always white with red edges, a splash of life against the dark gray lapel of his three-piece suit. He apparently wanted to project the solemn wisdom of a nineteenth-century business portrait, but it didn't work; he was 35 years old, looked 25, and acted 15.

He did succeed in being noticed. On this 90-degree July day when every other wholesale hardware salesman in the city was writing orders in a golf shirt, he was dressed as he always was—vest, carnation, and that wide smile people were never quite sure they could trust. Maybe that came from the same florist.

Bartley was alone in the office when Sterling entered with pompous flourish. He announced grandly, as though to a throng who had stood patiently for hours in the rain waiting for news from the throne, "I just got back from the coast." His neon smile flashed on and off. "Several manufacturers wanted me to come out and tour their plants. So I obliged them. Got to keep my suppliers happy.

"Just got in at noon," he went on breathily, leaning across Bartley's desk. "Flew first class. Always do. Nobody should have to travel coach. Criminal the way they pinch people into those seats. I won't put up with it!" He straightened up, folded his arms across his chest, leaned back a bit and said arrogantly, "And, of course, I don't have to put up with it. It's nice to go first class; first class all the way, any time I want to."

The smile lay unwavering, his head cocked to catch the first note of reply. What was it he wanted? A gasp of awe? A confession of envy? A congratulatory endorsement of his financial success? He posed motionless, but his eyes betrayed the confidence of his stiff smile. Behind Sterling's eyes Bartley saw a little boy jumping up and down, screaming for attention, saying, "See me! Be impressed! Think I'm okay. Like me! Like me! Tell me you like me!"

Bartley eked out a half-smile and said, "You peddlers really know how to live. We should all be so lucky." He laid down the ballpoint he had been gripping and massaged the indentation in his finger. "Seriously, though, I'm glad you came in. This being Friday, I didn't expect to see you."

"I try harder. That's why I'm number one." The smile flashed above his raised chin.

"Yeah. Well, like I was saying, we've got to have action on those window fans. Your shipping guy says they went out Monday. They're not here. We need 'em. Are you going to produce?"

"I'm on it." He grabbed the phone and dialed quickly. "June, put Charlie on. He is? That's no excuse!" To Bartley he said, "He's at a funeral," and back to the phone, "only kidding, June. Let me talk to Lloyd. Vacation? Who's running the place? Well, put him on, then, quick."

"Lloyd's on vacation, but I'll have your answer in a minute."

"Hey, Norm, trace the shipping of some window fans to Bartley Company. They went out on Monday. Call me back in five minutes. I need those fans over here this afternoon. I'm waiting. G'bye."

"Now, Bartley, we've got all afternoon to write new business. What else can I send you?"

"Nothing."

"You can't make money till you spend it, and I can't make any money till you spend it with me."

"Inventory's up, sorry to say. Slow summer."

"Maybe you're featuring the wrong stuff."

"I've got an ad for window fans in the paper tonight and not enough fans."

"I've taken care of that for you already."

"We'll see."

"What's that supposed to mean?"

"I need fans, not promises."

Color and hardness came into Sterling's face. "I've never let you down!"

"Not since the grass seed deal."

"That was my supplier's fault. I can't control that." He wiggled the knot of his tie, straightened his carnation, and rotated his college ring. "Besides, that was a long time ago."

"Two months."

"Well, your customers were understanding. You didn't lose any goodwill."

Bartley's response was slow, precise. "I'll be the judge of that. Goodwill is more important to me than it is to most people. I think maybe you don't really understand that."

Sterling was silent. It was the pungent silence of stifled anger and they were both relieved when the phone rang. The fans had not been shipped Monday, but would be sent over by company truck that afternoon. Bartley said, "Funny they couldn't figure that out in the fives times I called them this week," and silence again lay heavy.

Sterling pulled a flat white box from his briefcase and set it on the edge of Bartley's desk. "Macadamia nuts," he said, "from a special shop on the coast. Two days ago these nuts were on a tree in Australia. They're honey toasted. No place else fixes them this way. Very healthy, very expensive. You'll love 'em."

"Thanks."

"Wish I could stay. Got a lot more people to please before my day is over. See you again soon. Any time you need help, call me."

"Sure."

Sterling flashed his grin from the doorway and was gone. To Bartley, the room seemed twice as large.

Bartley set down his coffee cup and sighed, "It's great to be home, Hon. Thanks for the good dinner."

"Thanks for saying so," Linda replied, smiling. And then in a more serious tone, "You've been pretty quiet. Is it just Friday or is it something else?"

"There is something else but I've been trying to decide if it's worth talking about or not. It's a salesman. Personality clash, I guess you'd call it. I shouldn't bring something like this home with me."

"Why not?"

"Well, it seems like such a petty thing, yet this guy really annoys me. I was getting sarcastic with him this afternoon when I thought of that verse we had in Bible study about how we should build each other up with our talk. But he works so hard to build himself up, I just want to shoot him down. It's wrong, but . . . Do you think it would be okay to talk about it at Bible study tonight?"

"I don't know. When we started, this whole matter of

mutual support was discussed a lot, but no one has picked up on it much. People have pretty much stuck to the lessons." Linda thought a moment, then brightened. "Hey, this is the lesson in real life. Do it. Bring it up to the group tonight."

Sterling set down his coffee cup and sighed. His wife, Bunni, caught his eye and he looked away. She asked timidly, "What's bothering you?"

"Nothing."

"Oh, come on, big man. You can tell Bunni."

"There's nothing to tell."

"It's Friday night and you're not in your Friday night mood. Has it been a long week?"

"Every week is a long week."

"Tell me about your trip."

"There's nothing to tell."

"Did you bring back any of those good nuts?"

"Naw."

"I was hoping you would."

He pushed up from the table. "What's on TV?" he asked as he headed for the family room.

"Oh, Sterling, it's all reruns. Let's go out."

The family room door closed behind him.

Bible study was informal. Bartley had his usual spot on the floor, leaning against the end of the piano. After the coffee had been blown on and half sipped, and as the early banter was dying down, he spoke. "I want to ask about something we talked about last time—Ephesians 4:29 and this whole idea of building up others. How do you do that with someone who is making practically a full-time job of building up himself?"

Jerry spoke first. "Uh, yeah, sure. I thought we pretty well agreed last week we ought to build each other up. We all know it's hard but we do the best we can."

Ann added, "With God's help, of course."

"It isn't easy," Bartley said weakly. There were murmurs of agreement, then silence.

Ron said, "That verse bothered me this week, too. Especially when I listened to what I was saying to people. We shouldn't have studied that verse." There were chuckles from the group. He turned to Bartley. "We haven't given you any kind of answer and we need to. I guess maybe all of us need to understand this better. I sure do. Can you tell us some more of what's on your mind?"

"Sure. It's a salesman I do a lot of business with. The guy really bugs me and it bugs me that it bugs me. It's mostly just a matter of his style, I guess. He dresses fancy and struts around. In my mind I think of him as 'Mr. Mademoiselle.' Then he sprays his big grin around like it was a can of air freshener; but frankly, I gag on it. This guy really has a terminal case of self-importance and it gets to me."

In the quiet, he massaged the carpet with his hands and eyes. "Listen to the kind of things I'm saying about him right now. They certainly don't build him up, and think how embarrassed I would be if suddenly he was in this room hearing me talk about him. But I don't know how to change it. I could ask for another salesman but that wouldn't be fair to the guy—he's working hard to get ahead, and basically he's done a decent job of serving us. He's done better at that than I have at living like a Christian when I'm around him. So what do I do about it?"

Bunni turned the knob of the family room door slowly and gently pushed the door open—an inch, two inches. The light behind her wedged into the dark room. Sterling, lying on his back on the floor, was staring vacantly at the TV, vertical hold askew and the picture rolling flip, flip, flip.

He turned his head slightly to scowl at the sliver of Bunni that was visible. She froze. It was a stand-off of loneliness against loneliness; the fear of rejection against the fear of rejection.

She began pulling the door closed.

"Oh, for Pete's sake, if you're coming in, come in." It was gruff, but at least it was an invitation.

She entered slowly, eyes to the floor. "You want to watch TV?"

"There's nothing on. There's never anything on when I want to watch!"

"We could do something else."

"There's nothing to do."

"We could go to a movie."

"They're all rip-offs."

"It's nice out. Let's go somewhere."

"There's no place to go."

"We could go to a park—take some weenies and stuff."

"And watch everybody else have a good time?"

"It makes Bunni sad to see her big man so sad."

"Don't give me any of your pity—I don't need that! I'm a successful businessman. I'm a superstar of sales. I can take care of myself."

"But you're so sad."

Sterling rolled away from her and lay face down, his outstretched right arm gripping a chair leg. His breath came in fast, shallow bursts and his face, pressed against the carpet, was knotted into a hard, angry scowl. Every cell of his body strained to contain the emotional explosions detonating, one after the other, within him.

He remembered being laughed at in grade school. Boom!

He remembered finding his father, drunk, asleep on a neighbor's lawn. Boom!

He remembered the first time he asked Bunni for a date and she laughed in his face. Boom!

He remembered Bartley. Boom!

Slowly his grip on the chair relaxed and he forced in a long, deep breath. He felt drained, defeated—controlled by the pain of past rejection and fear of the future. Pinched between the two, the present was unbearable.

Bunni left the room as cautiously as she had entered.

Bartley was uneasy as he and Linda drove away from Bible study.

"Linda, are you sure this is the right thing to do? People just don't drop in unannounced on other people any more."

"Maybe that's part of what's wrong with society today. Besides, we discussed it, prayed about it, looked at all the Scripture we could find that pertained to it, and prayed again. The group agreed it's the thing to do."

"Easy for the group to decide what risks I should take."

"It's not a risk if the Lord says, 'Do it.' "

"I know," he murmured, "but . . . I'm scared."

"Me too. But, I guess we've got to decide if we go with how we feel or go with what we believe the Lord wants us to do. If it's the Lord's job for us now, it will work out fine."

"Yeah. I believe that. That's why we're going. But . . ."

Linda couldn't remember when he'd driven slower.

Bunni and Sterling were seated at the dinette idly leafing through magazines when their doorbell rang. Bunni jumped up to answer.

"Tell them I gave at the office," Sterling said sullenly. He winced when he recognized Bartley's voice, tentative but friendly.

"Hi, Bunni. We're the Browns—Bartley and Linda. We've met you at hardware dealer Christmas socials and places like that."

"Oh, sure, I remember. Yeah. This is a nice surprise."
She opened the screen door six inches and looked quickly
back for any sign of Sterling.

Bartley continued. "Hey, we don't want to be crashing
in on anything you're doing but, well, we were out this way
so we thought we might swing by and say hello."

"That's nice. Really nice. Come on in."

Sterling was still on the edge of his chair in the kitchen,
baffled, afraid, hopeful.

"Sterling!" Bunni said.

He entered the living room in standard form—hand
outstretched, hearty, tense. "This is a surprise! Welcome!
Yes, quite a surprise but a nice one! Sit down, sit down.
Bunni will get us some coffee, won't you, Bunni, please?
Want some coffee? Or a Coke? Make it a Coke, Bunni,
Coke and some crackers and cheese. This is nice to have
you drop by. So what brings you out this direction?"

Bartley fidgeted and plunged in. "Oh, we have a group
we meet with each week, not too far from here, so we were
over near here anyway, so it was like we were just more or
less in the neighborhood. But also, actually, the main
reason . . . that is the real reason, actually, I didn't feel too
good about today. About me, that is, which . . . I mean, I
thought I could have acted better. Well, actually, I was
pretty rude to you. I wanted to say to you I'm sorry for
that." It was awkward, but honest.

Sterling had never heard anything like it and it confused him. He wasn't sure if he was being complimented
or insulted, treated with respect or condescension.

Bartley continued. "You came in today, your usual
friendly self, ready to be helpful. I cut you down. Cheap
shots, basically. I was really out of line. That's why I say I'm
sorry."

Sterling glanced at Bartley and peeked at Linda from
the corner of his eye as his mind searched for a hidden

angle like a chess player whose opponent had suddenly left his king undefended. Could he trust Bartley? Why would a guy come over to say he's sorry about a little verbal punching in the course of business? Sterling could comprehend a salesman doing a humble bit, but the owner of seven stores? And to a salesman? It didn't make sense.

"Don't mention it," Sterling blurted. "No, that's not what I mean, uh, I'm glad you said it but you didn't need to. You hadn't hurt me. No harm, no foul; that's the way we play ball these days, isn't it? I had it coming about the grass seed. And the fans. They got over, didn't they?"

"Yes."

"I know they did. I checked on it." He shouted, "Bunni! Need any help?"

"Everything's ready," she said as she entered with a tray of snacks, which Sterling handed around.

Linda asked Bunni about a painting on the wall; Bartley and Sterling munched and sipped in silence.

Sterling hunted frantically for an ulterior motive to explain away Bartley's apology. He was afraid it was one more con job setting him up for rejection, and at the same time he sensed a chance for honest friendship and was afraid he would spoil it with his suspicion.

Bartley, relieved to be through the hard part, wondered what to do next. He prayed, "Lord, thank you for your presence and help. Give me the wisdom I need to do your work. Your will be done, Lord, your will, whatever it requires of me."

Sterling nudged open the silence. "Uh, it's really nice of you to stop over like this. Quite uncommon, though, I must say. Not that I don't like it, I do; but—quite uncommon." He grinned. "A cynical man might think you were up to something."

"Yeah, I can see why you might say that, as much

phoniness as there is around these days. But I don't think either you or I need to be phony."

Sterling heard it but his doubts remained. Again the smile and he said, "Still, it's an uncommon thing, an apology like that out of the clear blue sky. What's your angle? Are you *here* to sell *me*?"

"No, no. Nothing like that."

"Uh-huh," Sterling replied ever so slowly, still suspicious. "Well, tell me about this group you're in. Bridge club?"

"No. A discussion group, I guess you'd call it. We read and discuss."

"Books?"

"The Bible. Our purpose is to learn more about how the teachings of the Bible can help us in our everyday lives."

"Does it?"

"Yes, it's made a tremendous difference in life for me. And for Linda. I'd have to say my life is 100 percent different since I learned about God's plan for the world, about His design for human living, since I've allowed Him in my life as a full partner."

Here was the angle, Sterling thought with triumph. Everyone had one and now he knew Bartley's. And the angle was only religion. No big deal to counterplay that one. But to his surprise he heard himself say, "I'd like to hear some more about it. Bunni, listen to Bartley. I want you to hear this."

Bartley and Linda drove home quietly. It was late. Through the long discussion Sterling had been most cautious and skeptical, but serious, and with moments in which he showed what seemed to be honest longing.

The net effect seemed inconclusive to Bartley. "He may appreciate it, forget about it, or he may joke about me all over town. There's no way to know what's happening."

"I know what's happening."

"Yeah?"

"The Lord is working. Through us, even. And whatever course that takes is okay with me. The rest of the story is secure, because God is in control."

"Yeah!"

It was an ordinary day in mid-March, but Sterling knew something was different the moment he awoke. He hadn't awakened this happy since that time as a child when he had dreamed he was picking up money by the handful from all around the yard. That happiness had been shot to shreds the moment he'd rushed outdoors.

Wary of early morning exuberance ever since, he wondered if he could trust his feelings about this day. He edged to the window. A north wind from a menacing casket-gray sky scrubbed the leafless trees with cold rain.

It was the worst kind of day for a salesman—weather not bad enough to cancel appointments, but bad enough to slow you down and make you miserable between stops. Sterling had 12 stops on his list.

Sterling had been a Christian a month now. Driving back from one of his frequent lunches with Bartley he'd prayed, "Okay, Lord, I know I need you, and I want you in my life. I've sinned and I'm sorry. Forgive me. Please forgive me, that is. And if there is anything else that Bartley has taught me I'm supposed to say now, I include that too. Oh, yes, I believe in you. Amen."

He hadn't felt different but he believed differently. He was beginning to see that honesty was not a necessary evil but was intrinsically valuable, and that the customer was not a stooge to be manipulated but a colleague in the distribution process. He began to see himself, and Bunni, as worthwhile because of what *God* had done—created them as worthwhile—not because of what *they* had done.

And he behaved differently. Bunni said, "He's so mellow around the house I can't believe it. Now he's washing ᵗʰ ˋ dishes instead of throwing them." He asked his secre- ˋ , "How was your vacation?" and astonished her by staying to listen.

He hadn't been aware of feeling different; Bartley had said, "Don't worry about the feelings. Think right and act right and the feelings will take care of themselves." But this morning he felt happy, and that was uncommon enough to make him suspicious.

He enjoyed it yet puzzled over it through breakfast and on the way to work. He parked in the company lot and dashed across the street, zig-zagging with boyish enthusiasm among puddles to the produce market where he selected a carnation from the cut-flower case.

He still felt jaunty waiting at the checkout behind an elderly woman who bought one grapefruit, one banana, one lettuce wedge, and one small cluster of grapes. His ebullience was souring to impatience as he waited for her to carefully dig out coins and food stamps from a time-worn purse. He'd seen her a hundred times but had never before noticed the meticulous sewing of the patch upon a patch of her coat or considered any incongruity about her Atlanta Falcons umbrella.

He paid for the carnation and stood in the doorway, flower in hand, plotting his dash to the car. The lady stood placidly beside him, waiting for the rain to let up. She had all day to wait and he disliked her for it.

He had a sudden impulse to put on his carnation. As he pulled back the wet flap of his coat to pin it on the suit lapel above his heart he recalled suddenly an incident of long ago when he had stolen some prize postage stamps from his brother's collection. He hid them under one of Mother's flower pots and lied stubbornly about it until they were found, months later, dirty, water-damaged and worthless.

The old shame returned and he recognized it. He thought about his custom-tailored suits and his carefully rehearsed sales patter. He thought about the way he had used Bunni as an accessory in his wardrobe. He saw it all as a huge bouquet to conceal his feelings of inferiority, his phoniness, his cheap manipulations, his shabby retaliations and he knew he was tired of hiding.

He edged toward the lady and holding out the flower, said, "I just discovered I don't need this. I'd like for you to have it." He had no inkling then that she would become one of his and Bunni's best friends; at the moment it just seemed like the thing to do.

"Oh, I'm not sure."

"It's nothing much," he said, "but please enjoy it." He laid it on top of her bag and sprinted toward the car. "Thank you, Lord, for the goodness of hard lessons."

It rained all day, but Sterling didn't notice.

Discussion Questions

1. Do you know someone like Sterling? What part of that personality do you find most difficult to cope with?
2. Compare the two home scenes of Sterling and Bartley, particularly the way each interacted with his spouse.
3. Discuss the importance of the Bible-study group in Bartley's life. How important was it that Linda urge Bartley to talk about Sterling at Bible study?
4. Why do you think it was so difficult for Bartley to ask forgiveness of Sterling, and why was it so difficult for Sterling to accept Bartley's forgiving attitude?
5. Through Bartley's Christian witness, a change began to occur in Sterling. Cite evidence of this and discuss whether or not you think the changes are genuine.
6. Who is the Sterling in your life? The Bartley? The Ron?

Chapter Four

Walls: Barriers to Servant Friendship

We want close relationships, and we need them. That's the way we were created. Burke Dressen and Randy Jonas in chapter 1 believed life wasn't worthwhile without friendship. But, they kept bumping into walls they couldn't get through. You've probably faced those walls too, and you know others who face them now.

When we meet another person for the first time there is a bit of a wall between us, but we can hop right over it. Or we can raise that wall higher and we can create other walls to friendship either deliberately or by our lack of skill. For the most part, how easy or how difficult it is for us to develop friendships is determined by what we think and do, not by what the other person thinks and does.

Friendship doesn't happen automatically but it usually can happen easily and will happen frequently if we want it to. The walls can be overcome.

We will look at three types of walls to servant friendship. The first type we will call *implicit walls* because they exist in the natural world; for example, the imperfection of our abilities to see, hear, and think. Implicit walls are there; we can't eliminate them.

The second category we will call *reflexive walls*. These come from the early experiences of our lives, from our deeply engrained attitudes, and from the effects of sin on the human race—for example, fear or selfishness. We don't have to be hurt by these things but we probably are going to be.

The third category is called *created walls*. These are the additional walls that we erect ourselves, or encourage the other person to erect, through clumsy relational skills; for example, to be too pushy, to ask questions excessively, or to not share enough of our own ideas and experiences.

Implicit Walls

Let's begin with a quick investigation of the implicit walls. These are obstacles that are due to our limitations as human beings. For example, we don't hear everything the other person says. We never will, but this obstacle and all the others can be overcome.

Some of the confusion comes from the fact that our perception is imperfect. To perceive means simply to take something in through one of five senses: touch, sight, hearing, taste or smell. These senses aren't perfect. They reduce the accuracy of communication by misleading us in several ways.

We perceive things differently. Look at figure 2. What animal is it? A duck? A rabbit? Obviously, an animal cannot be both a duck and a rabbit. If you think this object is a duck and I think it is a rabbit, it will be difficult for us to understand each other as we talk about it because our comments are based on different assumptions.

Figure 2

We perceive what is not there. The grid of black squares in figure 3 illustrates this. Look at the "intersections" where the "streets" come together. Do you notice the gray spots that appear at the intersections except the one you are looking at? These gray spots appear to exist even though we know that they don't.

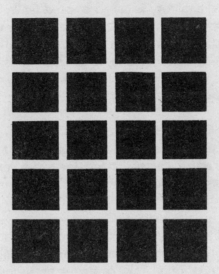

Figure 3

This illustrates that sometimes we perceive things that do not exist. Here our eyes have seemed to observe something that isn't there. In a similar way we sometimes misinterpret what we hear, touch, taste, or smell. The information that we work with, then, is not accurate.

We do not perceive what is there. This illustration uses the star and the dot that appear in figure 4.

★   ●

Figure 4

Hold the book vertically at about arm's length. Close, or put your hand over, your left eye and look at the star with your right eye. When you look at the star with the right eye, the black spot is also visible. Slowly bring the book closer to your face. At a point approximately 12 inches from your eye the black spot will no longer be visible when your right eye is looking at the star. As the book is brought closer in, the black spot will reappear.

The black spot has been there all the time, of course, but you haven't always perceived it. Under ordinary conditions this natural effect does not bother us but it does illustrate that our eyes, and our other senses, do not pick up all the information that is out there. With incomplete perception, understanding is incomplete.

It is hard to concentrate. Stop reading now and listen to all the sounds you hear around you. Each sound is competing for your attention. Think, too, about all of the other thoughts that have crossed your mind even as you have been reading this book. These are "sounds" from within that also compete for your attention. None of us finds it easy to keep our attention centered on one thing for more than a few seconds at a time without considerable conscious effort. We have the capacity to listen at 300 words per minute, yet most conversation is around 125 words per minute. That leaves a lot of empty space and each empty space is an opportunity for our minds to answer any of the distractions that are around us and within us.

Language itself doesn't work very well. Just as when two of us look at the same object and one of us may think it's a duck and the other may think it's a rabbit, in a similar way when we use a word we have quite different ideas about its meaning. If I say I would like to have a duck you might visualize a white domestic duck, a multi-colored wild duck, or a steaming, golden-brown roast duck on a platter. You might even think I want to go swimming. The word can also mean to dodge a blow or an unpleasant task, and is the name for a heavy cotton fabric and an amphibious military truck. Thousands of English words have more than a dozen meanings each. Even when we are precise in our own thinking and expression, the listener may choose a different meaning for our words than we intended.

Our own emotional involvement is a special kind of internal competition. Have you ever been so angry or so shocked with sorrow that you couldn't speak? Or have you ever been so surprised with good news that you literally were gasping for breath and speechless? Emotions do not need to be nearly that strong to interfere with accurate communication. Up to a point, emotional involvement increases our alertness and, with that, increases the accuracy of our communication. Then another point is reached at which the emotional intensity diminishes the accuracy.

We can't remove these walls because they are part of the natural world and of the human condition. But they do not need to handicap us. First we recognize them, and then we go on to develop communication skills that neutralize their effects.

Reflexive Walls

We tend to respond on the basis of previous experiences and this can allow new barriers, which we will call reflexive barriers, to form. They are created, but usually without our conscious intent and so quickly that it seems to us that they too are just a part of the natural world. They are not. They arise from the ordinary ways in which we organize, store and retrieve information and life experiences. We will need to learn relational skills that help overcome these walls.

Shadows of the past. Can you recall meeting a person for the first time and immediately disliking him or her without knowing why? Sure. This happens when something about that person reminds us of another person who hurt us in the past. That hurt, such as rejection, fear, or feelings of inadequacy when we compared ourselves to him or her, may have been unintentional. The other person may not have been aware of it; we may not have been aware of it. Probably this new person neither has awareness of it nor has anything to do with that old hurt. But our attitudes toward him or her have been influenced already, a barrier to relationship. This too is an emotional involvement, but one that may never have been appropriate and that is unnecessary now.

Stereotypes. These are based on the notion that people who are similar in one way must be similar in other ways. For example: all psychologists are flaky and all professors are absentminded. Those characteristics are true only part of the time! Generalizations like these are based on such things as race, religion, occupation, nationality, age, geographic location, physical size, name, color of hair and so on. This is a good time to remember what Disraeli said: "All generalizations are false, including this one." Because what might be true of one house painter or Presbyterian or redhead or Bolivian will not necessarily be true of another.

Most stereotypes have had a shred of truth in them at some point in history, but all of them can be destructive. They may cause us to avoid other persons or to treat them in some very general way rather than as the one-of-a-kind creation each of them is.

When we respond to a new person on the basis of stereotype, we will be off the target in most respects. We should seek to know each person as a unique and special individual.

Selfishness and self-centeredness. Our human inclination, the result of sin, is to put ourselves first and to try to adjust the world to revolve around us. That's selfishness. Humanistic pronouncements have reinforced that, bombarding American society with messages to "look out for number one"; "pull your own strings"; "get yours." These messages appeal to the sinful nature within us. The methods seem to work in the short run but they contradict God's order and therefore cannot lead us to joy and meaning in life.

It's hard not to be selfish because our direct contact with reality is through perception that is self-centered. Wherever we are, we are aware of ourselves and of the people and objects in our immediate environment. All that we know about the world is filtered through our perception, and that perception is contaminated by our built-in selfishness.

To demonstrate our self-centered tendencies, imagine driving a car along a highway and a pheasant suddenly flies into your path and is struck. Would you say, "The car hit a pheasant," or "I hit a pheasant"? Most people would say, "I hit a pheasant," because while driving we make the car an extension of ourselves. Its bumpers, sidepanels and tires become, in a sense, our outer "skin," sensitive to the "touch" of the road, the wind, and other objects, much the way our physical bodies are sensitive to our immediate surroundings.

Now, let's extend our awareness of being self-centered beyond the outer extremities of the car to the farthest reaches of our physical sense, beyond taste and touch to smell, and farther to hearing, and to the farthest-reaching sense, sight. As with the car, we tend to extend ourselves to the farthest extremities of our experienced environment, and that extension embraces all things within our environment, including people.

Our self-centered experience has a built-in tendency to become selfish—to be so preoccupied with self that the needs of others are not noticed or attended to. Remember the two stories in chapter 1? Burke Dressen was seen by his customer, Rich, as an object that changes tires. Randy was seen by his customer, Fred, as a person, not just as an object that fills prescriptions. Of the two customers, Fred was the more unusual because he quickly moved beyond his self-centeredness to other-centeredness, a key step in servant friendship.

Communication is the process that makes such a step possible. All of us, when we first encounter another individual, see that individual as an object in our environment. We acquire a first impression of the individual, an impression that is inside us—an extension of ourselves, rather than outside us—other than ourselves. But the nonverbal and verbal communication of the other begins to alter that impression. If we remain self-centered we offer great resistance to any change in the impression. Burke's nonverbal behavior gave Rich a clue that this tire-changing object had some personal problems; but these problems, thought Rich, should not have interfered with its tire-changing function. Of course, had Rich known the severity of the problems, he might have reacted differently. By contrast, Fred had established a pre-set in his own mind to notice that the prescription-filling object was a person and he responded to the nonverbal clues in Randy's behavior, adjusting his first impression of Randy more and more as communication between them proceeded.

We overcome selfishness gradually. It begins by recognizing the self-centered nature of our life experience. It uses good communication as a process of sharing worlds of experience, adjusting initial impressions, and allowing the center of the universe to be outside oneself. As we listen to and observe other people we become less self-centered. As we seek to put their needs before our needs we gain confidence in our capacity to be servant friends. Most important are the things we do to grow in Christian maturity—looking at Christ and seeking to practice His patterns for living.

Fear is a normal and desirable signal that we might get

hurt. If we refuse to be a servant friend when we could, we are indulging in a particular form of selfishness.

Christine knows that she should pay a visit to her friend Ruth in the hospital, but she can't overcome her morbid fear of sickness and death. She sends flowers instead.

John crouches a little lower in the pew one Sunday a month when an appeal comes from the pulpit for volunteers to visit the juvenile detention center. What, after all, does he have in common with the young people there? What could he say to them? Sometimes he imagines telling one of them about Jesus: At first, the youngster is very receptive, but suddenly the daydream changes and all the kids are laughing at John. He decides to let someone else volunteer. After all, he thinks, ministering to juveniles is not his calling.

Steve and Ralph are in the same small fellowship group. Steve has a problem he's been carrying around for years and he needs to talk to someone about it. He comes to Ralph, thinking that Ralph might be trustworthy and willing to listen. Ralph cares a lot about Steve, but he can't tolerate the thought that Steve might not be as spiritually mature as he appears to be. Ralph interrupts Steve, saying, "I probably don't know enough to be able to help you. You ought to talk to the pastor about that."

Christine, John, Ralph, and probably all of us at one time or another, are saying, "I don't want to get involved." We may anticipate something good and rewarding from offering ourselves to others in servanthood friendship, but we are also apprehensive of the possible hassle or pain in such encounters. Often we fear most that which we desire most, and the result is indecision, inaction, and a sense of failure and guilt. With every encounter there are three possible outcomes: acceptance, rejection, or indifference. We all desire acceptance and fear rejection or indifference. If acceptance were guaranteed the world would be populated with nothing but servant friends. Fear of rejection or indifference keeps most of the world's potential servant friends in the closet.

You can prevent fear from controlling your life. Get information, practice skills, request the counsel and support of others, and move out with God's partnership in your life, for then you cannot fail. You may still feel fear, but it won't matter to you.

We remove or lower reflexive walls through conscious effort at better self-understanding and acceptance of others. These are tasks at which we continue to improve throughout our lives. We begin by centering on Christ and using relational skills to know the other person and to share ourselves honestly so they may know us.

Created Walls

Created walls are barriers we raise, or cause the other person to raise, by our low level of competence. Even when we have good intentions, as we do most of the time, we are likely to make mistakes.

We call the following "Verbal Villains." As you read them don't say, "Oh, I know somebody just like that!" Rather, ask yourself, "Do I ever do this?" If so, learn to recognize that behavior so you can change it in the future.

There was a town, years and years ago, that was founded on the principle that its people ought to help one another. All the original settlers were selected on the basis of their enthusiasm for helping their friends and neighbors. They named the town "Helpful," and it was a beautiful place in the midst of mountain grandeur somewhere in the Wild West. This is the way it was as told to me by a great grandchild of one of the original settlers of this imaginary town of Helpful.

It was the summer of eighteen-seventy-something and Jared and Maybelle Purvy were two people with a wagonload of stuff among thousands headed west across the prairie. They got along fine, surviving dust, ruts, bugs, fear, naiveté and boredom, until they came to Lizard River, which was roaring from recent rain. All the wagons forded successfully, but the Purvys broke a wheel midstream and capsized. Jared and Maybelle jumped, swam to shore, and watched everything they owned rush swiftly downstream. They spent two days scrounging along the banks hoping to salvage a few things, then trudged, ragged and weary, eight miles into Helpful.

And help they were offered! The good citizens meant well, but . . . What do you think? Were responses like these really beneficial to Jared and Maybelle? The first person they met was the self-styled village philosopher.

Plato X. Platitude, the guru. He was the master of a million clichés. As a young man he vowed to think only threadbare thoughts and speak only in banal generalities. He succeeded. He told them, "Things always get better. Keep a stiff upper lip. This too shall pass away. The bluebird of happiness will fly into your life again. Into each life some rain must fall, but every cloud has a silver lining. God hath mysterious ways, His wonders to perform. Keep looking up."

Sergeant Cracko D. Whip, drill sergeant in the Helpful volunteer cavalry. Cracko was a friendly enough guy, but since he knew the answer before he heard the question, it was only natural that he was a little impatient. "There's only one way to handle this," he ordered. "First, admit that you're totally wiped out by this thing. Number two, you both have to get jobs. Three, wire home for money. Four, go to the livery and rent a horse so you can take a job on a ranch. Then, number five, you . . ."

Delphinium Delight, the florist. She could gush more gallons per minute than Miracle Spring, the hot bath place over at Radium Gulch. Like she said to Maybelle, "Every-thing's goin' to be all right. Look at you now, still with that gorgeous, simply gorgeous, hoop skirt! And your smile!

Law me, but you have the widest, prettiest, most perfect smile that ever came through this town. Isn't it just wonderful to have such a pretty dress and pretty smile!"

Bristles Gish, the sign painter. "Well, folks, your whole problem is, you're Tenderfoots. Green-as-grass, soft-as-a-baby's-belly Tenderfoots. Now, that's okay by me, don't get me wrong, but you got to get Seasoned. It takes a few years to get a little Grizzled, if you know what I mean. A Native would know those things that an Outsider just hasn't learned. You need to be Experienced Settlers."

Bristles thought he solved problems by naming them. It is easy to put labels to situations or persons—much easier than helping change things—but the label doesn't change conditions, does it?

Mrs. Mariah Henn, boardinghouse proprietor. "Dear me, children, you need help! Just come with me over to my boardinghouse. I'm Mrs. Henn, but all my boarders call me 'Mother.' There, there, little Maybelle. Don't you worry your pretty head for a minute. The two of you are coming home with me. I'll take care of you."

The Incomparable Elmo, magician. The incredible prestidigitator was passing through Helpful on his way to the big time over at Whistling Ridge the day Jared and Maybelle straggled into town. He said, "Don't worry about it. Everything's going to be all right."

He wants you to think he can make problems vanish with a quick "presto-chango." How often has that command been useful to you? He fools himself, but he doesn't help others.

Professor Stigma Froid, mind reader and analyst. "My word, lad," he said, his 10 fingertips pressed lightly on Jared's skull, "the emanations of your cerebellum tell me you've come upon hard times. I don't need to notice your tattered, mud-caked clothing to know that. Emanations—yes, it's all there in the emanations. I alone am gifted to know the language of the mystic, ethereal electric emana-

tions and to interpret them for the ill-informed. Ah, there is
so much more I could explain to you about your sordid
longings, about your repressed conflicts, and only for the
paltry sum of . . ."

Strather Mathis, memory whiz. "Think of this. 'I will lift
up mine eyes unto the hills, from whence cometh my
help.' That's Psalm 121:1. Another good Psalm is 100;
also 97 and 98. They're all good in times of discourage-
ment. It says in 1 Chronicles 16:11, 'Seek the Lord and his
strength, seek his face continually.' Paul wrote to the
Corinthians 'stand fast' and 'be strong.' He said 'stand
fast' in many of his epistles—to the Philippians, to the
Thessalonians, to the Galatians. I'm not sure about Colossians, but it must be important. The Greek word is *steko*.
I've had perfect attendance at Sunday School since the
church was organized."

*Mystic Margo, swami, seer, and part-time rain dancer
(summer only).* She liked her work because she could get
finished early—she didn't have to stay around and see
how things turned out. Or didn't turn out. "It's an easy
job," she said, "if you have plenty of imagination and
don't care about results."

She told Maybelle, "If you let this thing get you down,
it will be the worst thing that happens to you. If you go
back East you'll be kicking yourself for the rest of your life!
Two weeks from now you'll be saying, 'Why, oh why, did
we head back home?' Believe me, I can see how it's going
to come out!"

Phineas J. Ferret, the detective. "I'll get to the facts of
the case if it's the last thing I do," Phineas roared. He threw
his hat to the floor and thumped a stubby finger on Jared's
chest. "You sure your wagon wasn't overloaded? What
kind of wood was the wagon axle made of? How many
spokes in the wheels? Were you driving mules or horses?
Are you sure you fed them proper? Where were you on
the night of the fourteenth?"

Mr. "X," the hangman. He wasn't really a citizen. The good townsfolk were determined that things would never come to the point of needing a hangman. But Mr. "X" just stuck around, camped in a cluster of scrub oak upon which the buzzards roosted, and together they scanned the town with sad eyes and gloomy souls, hoping for a better day when things would be really, really bad. When Jared and Maybelle trudged down the dusty road past his camp he called out with a weary sort of scolding, "It's your own fault. Anybody else would have checked their wheels carefully before putting into that river. You can blame the river or blame God or say whatever you want, but it's your own fault and it serves you right. Maybe this will learn you something!"

Brother Piety N. Bluesky, free-lance saint. "Praise be, brethren, the Lord is blessing you. He chastens you because He loves you. Rejoice in the loss of your worldly clutter. Sound the cymbal of thanksgiving for this tragedy."

Sister Joy S. Verboten, free-lance prophet. "Shame be to you. The judgment of the Lord is upon you. His wrath is visited upon your sins. Dark is the path you trod, for His avenging angel demands your repentance. Fall in fear."

Hans R. Calloused, the foreman. Now there's some kind of honcho. There is nothing you can think of but what he'll come up with a job that'll take your mind off it! Like he told Jared, "Boy, you've had some tragedy, that's so. Now, you go to work; it'll take your mind right off your troubles. Go to punching cattle. Ride the range. There ain't nothin' like a few saddle sores to make you feel like a new man!"

Lathum R. Papyrus, the historian. Aside from the times when he got a little apoplectic when the young folks called him "Dusty," or even "Musty," he was as friendly as a chipmunk—a man who'd give you the time of day. Of course he could keep you there till your eight-day clock ran down, but he meant well, and he did know stories. Like he said to Maybelle, "Daughter, that river runs high in the spring and low in the fall. There was a time, way back, oh, maybe 20, 30 year ago, when the antelope would come down there in the fall. Me, I was a trapping back then, and me and my partner we would . . ."

Floogle Barnwell, zealot. "I'll take charge here. Let's get . . . no, that wouldn't work. Well, we could . . . uh, that might not be best either. We should . . . er, uh . . . Hey! Let's . . . no . . . or, . . . Shucks, I don't know. I guess it's hopeless." Floogle's best feature was his strong back.

Well, those are some of the characters of the town of Helpful. Sadly, their only sin was over-enthusiasm. "We just tried too hard, I guess," Letha Bindweed observed. The town disbanded.

The pilgrims went their separate ways, settling one here, another there, but their descendants live on and prosper. You know some of them. Are you one too?

The most deceptive thing about the Verbal Villains is that each is partly right. They say some good things. Under some conditions, their statements could be valuable. But early in Jared and Maybelle's time of need there were better things to have said, better ways to have helped.

The Verbal Villains are ineffective methods often used by persons who have good intentions to be helpful. The barriers they create are mistrust, misunderstanding and cautiousness, and it is hard to overcome them.

But there are other barriers that can be created from behaviors which are even more hurtful, those communication styles that the Bible explicitly condemns, namely: lying, slander, gossip, malicious talk, quarrelling, cursing, vulgarity and rage. The Bible, from front to back, clearly teaches that such behaviors have no place in the life of the Christian.[1] The consequences are extreme: to knowingly engage in any of these behaviors is to deliber-

ately disobey God's way of life. These behaviors are con-
demned because they are destructive. The destruction is
particularly damaging to relationships because it hurts the
other person.

The other person will probably become defensive,
prefer to avoid us, and may seek to retaliate. In addition,
the practice of these behaviors erodes our personal sense
of worth, causes shame and guilt if we are sensitive to our
consciences, and makes us vulnerable to doing further
wrong behavior.

For most Christians these obviously hurtful behaviors
are not as great a problem as the Verbal Villains which are
more subtle in their damage. The best approach is to
displace the wrong behavior that our human nature would
lead us into with the qualities and skills that are pleasing to
God: to compensate for implicit walls with good skills, to
overcome reflexive walls by getting to know the real person, and to avoid created barriers by becoming aware of
the pitfalls of various ineffective relational styles.

Discussion Questions

1. Identify the three walls that hinder servant friendship
   and give an example of each. What walls are most
   likely to be part of your life?
2. What do you see as the most effective way to move
   beyond one's self-centeredness to other-centeredness?
3. Give examples of the part that fear plays in hindering
   you from being a servant friend. How might you be a
   better servant friend to someone in the coming week?
4. Discuss the "Verbal Villains" and pick out the one (or
   ones) most familiar to you.

Note

1. See, as examples, these verses: Leviticus 19:16; Psalm 15:2,3; 34:13;
Proverbs 6:16-19; Matthew 12:35-37; Ephesians 4:29-31; Colossians 3:8; 2
Timothy 2:23,24; James 1:26; 4:11; 1 Peter 3:10.

Chapter Five

Is There Anyone Out There Who Cares?

by Daniel J. Siemasko

I wasn't sure where to find it or how much I could expect to get, but I had to start looking for someone who cared. I had to have a friend.

My name is Brad Obitz, and I'd like to tell you what happened one painful weekend a year ago. This will seem like fiction because we don't usually see killings in nice, caring families like mine; but Obitz caring is different. We care about ourselves and our rights, we care about pushing back, we care most of all to fight. I was as much at fault as anyone.

Friday, after school: My mother knuckled sharply on the three books she had put in front of me. "Care! Can't you care? Think of what's happening to you!"

This was the kind of treatment I had grown to expect from Mom. She was on the attack again and I was tired of the everyday battle. I looked down and sized up the books: Christian junk, Christian junk, and one on positive something-or-other.

"You're 17 now, almost a man. All I want is for you to grow up and be a loving somebody."

"Like the man you married?" Then I wished I hadn't said that. I didn't want to fight anymore. I was becoming the ugliness she made me out to be. But neither did I want to be her weakling.

"Why, your father has given you dah-dadah . . ."

I had a special way of listening to Mom. An automatic mechanism filtered out the superfluous and tuned in every opportunity for a biting reply.

". . . dah-dah-dah . . . What do you think this life you've been given is for? For the fun of it?"

An affirmative would only have prompted more enemy fire. It took a clenched jaw to keep it in. I braced myself with a stiff arm on the sill and a straight stare out the window. She spoke to the side of my face: "You have to care. Everybody cares-dah-dah-dah . . ."

All she cared about was that I cared about what she cared about. She wanted this life I'd been given.

"Look at me, 38 and going to school. Why? Because I have learned, even at this late date, that you have to make it happen for yourself."

My scream was only inside as I thought, "Then why are you trying so hard to do it for me?!"

With her fist pumping the cadence of the words like a concert conductor, Mom reached her finale. "You-have-to-care. Everybody cares . . . even jellyfish!"

With the exclamation point came contact. What at another time would have felt like a touch on the shoulder was now a push. In an instant the ugliness I hid deep came bolting to the surface: the surge of hate, the fear of the surge, the prayer for the fear. I raised a heavy potted plant high as Mom repeated, "You-have-to . . ." But she didn't get the last word out. She stopped to watch her most carefully groomed bonsai crash against the bookshelf.

She started up again. "That proves you don't care about anything! It's just what I'd expect from you. You're hopeless-dah-dah-dah . . ."

Two things shocked me. First, I wasn't holding and hiding any ugliness or cowardice. I didn't feel like the uncaring nothing that Mom described me to be.

Second, I was shocked to find a prayer in me, even a millisecond prayer. I had never liked that—for real and on time—before. She kept on, but I felt my fight with her was over.

Saturday, after dinner: Looking back, I see that I wasn't the only suffering person in our caring home.

"Don't give me that. I do care!" Dad snapped at Mom.

I was having my dessert just around the corner in the living room, closer than they thought. Odd, but Mom wouldn't fight with Dad in front of me.

"If you did you wouldn't be sitting there like the king," Mom said, coming from the kitchen.

"Nine to five, five days a week, I care," he said. "I worry about keeping our bellies full, our feet soled, our house warm, our bills paid—basic things like that." She was back in the kitchen.

Were these two together adults telling it like it is? No, they were two adults together avoiding telling it like it is. From all the pieces I could put together now, I could see why my father was so uptight. He felt trapped. There was no way to tell his wife, surely not the kids, not even a way to tell himself; after all, he was the head of the household. According to Obitz tradition he had to provide. I could see he wasn't all pleased with Mom's going to school. Yes, he encouraged her to get out of the house and into the world, to work and to help; but to work on a new career without helping to support the household, no, that's not what he meant. (He'd give his right arm for a chance to get re-schooled out of Prissen Precision Machinery.) He couldn't outright say, "I can't provide." So expressing himself, without telling it all, had him speaking in strange loud contortions: "If there's anyone here who doesn't care about anybody in this house, it's not me!"

My mother came storming out of the kitchen and began stacking the plates. She knew she was being accused. She nested the pudding bowls together and clunked them down on the plates. "That's not what I meant," she said as she snatched the tablecloth from under the pile of plates and crumpled it into a handful.

All Mom wanted was some help clearing the table after dinner, maybe an offer to do the dishes, basic things like that. Dad took a lot for granted.

"If I didn't care about you," Dad continued while I came by to drop off my dish, "—or about the kids—do you think I'd keep my miserable job?"

Mom yanked the dish from me and dropped it into the suds. She took her damp cloth to the table. I watched the two of them.

"Eighteen, going on 19 now"—I knew what Dad was going to say. This thing was always a year older than I. Dad would often misguess my age, but never the time he served at Prissen. "Eighteen-and-a-half years at a job I despise, but am stuck with. And not for me. For you! I do this for my family."

Mom looked like she was sanding the formica off the tabletop.

"Would I come so close to insanity if I didn't care?" A glance from her would have helped. Nothing.

I watched his arms strain, his fists grow under cover. "It's you! You wouldn't be driving me nuts if *you* cared!" His pockets held the force. "You, too," he shot at me.

Strange—his normal treatment but without my usual quarrel.

Doing your duty is another way of caring. Again, after you do what you have to do, the rest of the time is yours to be as uncaring as you like. It's point-system love, a variation of "I gave at the office." What a convenient way to love. You give once and then you're free not to give again.

Family, don't expect anything—father cared at the office.

Why do I get so cynical? Because not being taken care of hurts—especially when you think that the caring you need is coming, but doesn't.

Back then I didn't know what I needed. I just felt the ache from whatever was missing. It was so hard for me to get past "I need," that I never got to fill in the blank, "I need _____."

My family turned on the fanfare: "And now, here's _____, just what you need. This is caring!" The glittering curtains spread—but it wasn't what I needed; it wasn't caring. And now, not only do I still have my first unidentified longing, I also have the added load of disappointment. Since others were so sure this would satisfy, but it didn't, confusion jumped on. Since I couldn't say why their caring didn't help, frustration piled on. And since pure parental caring couldn't do the trick, hopelessness on top of that. Where did I get the notion that I could be cared for more completely?

Saturday, after Mom and Dad's fight, Chipper, supposedly the Obitz caring champion, and I went at it.

(Chipper's the name my 14-year-old sister prefers to Charlotte. Mom used to say her do-good daughter reminded her of Dad, a chip off the old block. Dad liked the connection and called his thin blonde offshoot "Chipper." And Chipper liked the way her dad shined everytime he said it. Besides, she hated "Charlotte.")

"Well, I'll tell you what, Charlotte"—brothers have a way with words—"you show me one person who really cares for you and I'll do the dishes." Touché.

She wasted no time: "Dad cares, Mom cares." The dishcloth came sailing my way. "That's two, so you can do the supper dishes too." Not bad for 14.

"No." I grabbed her hand and inserted the towel. "I mean *really* cares." Of course, I had no idea of what real caring was. I didn't think there was anything there after you peeled away selfishness. But that didn't stop me. "Parents love you for themselves. Otherwise they'd feel guilty. Show me the real stuff."

"You wouldn't know the real stuff if it hit you in the face," Chipper said.

"But since I'm the expert in non-caring, I don't think I'd miss caring if it stood in front of me with a dishrag."

"You could try caring yourself—but of course you wouldn't know when you had it." She was sharp tonight.

"Why should I try?" I asked.

"To be a better person. Try it, you'll like it."

"I tried once," I laughed. Although this was our usual fighting action I wasn't caring to hurt.

"Name one person you ever tried caring for," the Chipper challenged.

"Cindy Britanik," I answered quickly. I still had to be fast.

"The smart girl who dumped you after going steady with you for four whole days?"

"Yep, the same one. Actually, I was uncaring and Cindy knew it." Thought I'd shake the Chipper with my honesty, some upper-teen experience, and a bit of exaggeration for effect: "All I wanted was sex."

My sister turned away. I didn't see the gulp, but it was there.

"Oh, I cared," I said, continuing to lunge forward. "I did all the things she expected from a steady, to get what I wanted. It was as selfish as stealing."

"Worse."

"See? So when you, Mom, Dad or whoever comes around with the caring bit, I'm only being smart, like Cindy."

"So we're all the same to you?"

"No, you're not all the same"—time for the kill. I found the fighting words in my mouth, but they only hurt me when they came out. "There are some people I don't care for more than others."

"So nobody really cares."

"And you do the dishes, Charlotte."

Chipper should have been the best chance I had of finding a friend in our family, but she was too occupied being Dad's second edition and Mom's Number-One-Caring-Person-in-the-Whole-World. Mom was too busy keeping our relationship unfriendly. I once called Dad "my friend"—"I'll show you your friend; I'm your father!" he exclaimed.

What kind of a caring friendship was I after? Now that a year has passed I think I know what goes in the blank: a someone. I'll try to be specific:

I needed caring, not curing. There are times when campaigns and pat answers just won't do. I needed a break from being the kid who just hasn't learned yet, from being the patient for those who want to play doctor, from being the darkness for those who only care to shine.

I needed someone with time enough for me. I needed someone I could open up to, unhurriedly.

I needed someone who respected what I was and met me there. I needed to know there was caring beyond manipulation.

I needed someone who believed in my hoping. Someone who thought, maybe even more than I, that these things were possible.

I needed someone I could trust. Someone who would show me my shortcomings carefully. Someone I could be honest with—one who wouldn't laugh when I was serious, but who laughed a whole lot the rest of the time.

As independent as I act, *I needed someone who could see how I fit into this world.* Although I'm upset at society's direction, I'm distressed over being left out. This someone could help to put me on *my* tracks, understanding what's important to me, applauding at the right times.

I needed someone to comfort me when I failed.

With all these I-needs, I needed someone to tell me I wasn't completely selfish, to believe I cared about others too. I needed someone who knew how uncaring I had been and how undeserving I was but who wouldn't rub my face in it. One who still cared enough to want to know me better.

Christians said I needed Jesus Christ. They were right, but back then I thought that Christianity was just a fairy tale and I knew I couldn't survive this life on just that. I needed an arms-and-legs, head-and-heart person to prove to me there was such a thing as caring.

Then I met Shawnee, and she was my someone until my someone was Jesus. She listened, she accepted, she taught. I wasn't the Lord's only unique case, she'd joke. She helped me believe what I heard in my prayers; she entrusted me and my cares to Jesus.

Funny, once I thought my cares had nothing to do with caring. There should have been two separate words: one for my emptiness, and "caring" for why one helps an old lady across the street.

Shawnee gave me a card on which she had written "Humble yourselves, therefore, under God's mighty hand, that he may lift you up in due time. Cast all your [care] upon him because he cares for you—1 Peter 5:6,7." God's *caring* is for our *cares*! The longings we have are meant to get the Royal Treatment.

My Phillips translation says, "You can throw the whole weight of your anxieties upon him, for you are his personal concern." If only my parents and Chipper could hear this Bible quoter now!

Sunday morning. I was taking the family to church. This was a year ago, remember—before Shawnee, before Jesus.

My driver's license was a week old. Dad was looking awkward in the passenger seat and Mom the same in the back. My sister was uneasy seeing me with so much control.

Again this morning our family was into caring, the word. I had already decided this was my last. This was the end. I wanted everyone to speak their last piece so I was pushing: "Why should I care if Mom does all my caring for me?"

"If I ever talked about my mother like that when I was a kid, I'd be thrown out on the road," my father said.

"If *you* cared, I wouldn't have to do your caring for you," Mom answered me from the back seat.

I was just getting onto the expressway. "Dad, what else am I to you besides a big-mouthed kid?"

"Like your mother says, you're stubborn and selfish. You won't amount to anything because you don't care about what you're supposed to do."

I had the car up to 60 quickly. The faster the better. "What am I to *you*, Mom?"

"A jellyfish."

"About that smart, too," injected the Chipper.

"What else am I to you, Charlotte?"

"You're a sad case, brother. With so many who need love, you use yours to hurt."

Trees were going 65 now, the other way. There were few guardrails. "What else am I to you?"

"A loser, brother. Bet you never had a 'thank you' come your way."

"What else am I to you?"

"A pain in my side. While I'm out to share my goodness with others, you're always there sticking it to me."

I had the accelerator to the floor—that's not saying much for our old gray economy wagon. "What else am I to you, anyone?"

Dad answered last: "Look at you, the way you keep asking that question. You're filled with hate. You're no good the way you are."

As I whipped the car onto the exit ramp I heard it all—the screaming, the hollering, the fighting—and I knew it was over for me. Mom, Dad, and the Chipper were pleased to be at church on time. I let them off at the front door and I drove straight to the bus station and boarded the first one leaving: destination—someone who cares like a friend.

Discussion Questions

1. Describe 17-year-old Brad Obitz and what was going on inside him during the weekend he described.
2. Discuss the mother's verbal interaction with Brad and with her husband.
3. When Brad is talking about his mother, then later with his father, he hints that he's "heard it all a hundred times before." Do you think this is typical in family communication, and if so, how can it be avoided or remedied?
4. What do you think of Brad's idea on "point-system love, a variation of 'I gave at the office'"? He thinks his father is silently saying, "Family, don't expect anything—father cared at the office." Do you think his is a valid criticism?
5. What is Brad's feeling toward his sister and toward her place in the family? Have you seen that attitude before?
6. What is your assessment of Brad's list of "I needed . . ." beginning with *I needed caring, not curing*?

Chapter Six

Doors: Skills for Entering Friendship

We'd want to offer Brad Obitz better friendship than he found within his family. To do that we'd need skills—the open doors through which we can move toward understanding another person and his or her circumstances. This chapter presents skills that are usually important in the early part of a servant friendship. But first a reminder—skills are nothing without an underlying commitment of love.

The first few seconds of an encounter with another person are packed with activity: the two of you establish whether or not you will talk more and what you want from each other. You may learn the other person's name. This is the "contact phase," lasting anywhere from a fraction of a second to a few minutes. What happens during this time is very important because it sets the tone for what may come later. If you show that you care and can be trusted, the other person will probably decide to let you enter further into his or her life. If you are inept in this phase, the other person will probably resist your efforts to be a friend.

Contact Behaviors

Servant friendship, an expression of love, requires communication, which begins with "contact behaviors"—little things such as a nod, eye contact, saying "hello"—by which you and the other person show whether or not you are interested in further conversation. Because they come at the beginning of the interaction they have high impact—for better or worse.

Through these brief messages we communicate such things as "I'm interested in you" or "I'm busy now" or "I don't trust you," messages that strongly affect what happens next. These messages may be sent either verbally, in words, or nonverbally, using media such as gestures, distance, posture, timing, tone of voice, facial expression, or touch. Contact behaviors can open the other person to more interaction or close them to the idea. Here are examples of each of the four combinations:

Openers: Effective Contact Behaviors

Nonverbal	Verbal
Smile	Routine small talk
Wave, beckoning gestures	A greeting
Handshake	Introduce self
"Ahem!" hum, whistle	Non-threatening questions
Tap body, touch, hug	Honest compliment
Wink, nod	Use their name
Give a "helping hand"	Comment on the present
Remove barriers such as	situation
furniture or sunglasses	Explain what's going on

Closers: Ineffective Contact Behaviors

Nonverbal	Verbal
Frown, glare, angry look	Sarcasm, insults, even in
Keep doing something else	fun
Take over their activity	Derogatory remark
Yawn, sigh, look at watch	Brag
"Don't care" posture	Too personal questions
Gruff tone of voice	Be phony
Turn away	Change the subject
Fidget, high nervousness	Cheap advice, cliché
	answers
	Condescension

Improvement of this skill begins with awareness of what you do now and what effect your words and actions have on others. This week pay close attention to your contact behaviors to see if your signals clearly convey genuine interest in others. If they don't, your attitudes or behaviors—perhaps both—need to change.

Now, a brief word on behalf of small talk: it's valuable, it shows interest and caring and it is usually enjoyable. As the first step in many conversational journeys it often leads to talking about more important things. Improve your skill; use it. It does not matter if you ring or knock; if you show you're interested in other persons they'll open the door.

Assessment

As you listen to the other person you routinely assess what he says, asking yourself questions such as, "What does this person want from me?" or "What does this person need now?" You may not think consciously about this process but it is something that you probably have always done.

Almost any situation can be put into one of five categories: request for physical help, request for information, request for understanding/involvement, inappropriate interaction, or the expression of anger. It is valuable to learn to recognize the type of need or demand because we respond differently to each kind of need. We shall consider each of these categories and include suggestions about how to deal with them when the friendship is established, long after the contact phase and the initial assessment.

Request for physical help. The other person wants or needs assistance. He may directly seek help from you, such as a church secretary saying, "Would you help me fold these bulletins?" Or the request may be stated indirectly, as "I just don't know how I'll ever get all these bulletins folded before I have to leave this afternoon!"

Indirect requests are a way of reducing the risk of

rejection. If we ask for help we may not get it—a bit of rejection. Some people don't want to run the risk of being rejected so rather than ask directly they hint around, hoping that someone will recognize their need and offer help. As we become more sensitive to other persons we will begin recognizing these indirect requests for physical help, information, or understanding/involvement.

When physical help is needed we should consider providing it. Many physical needs and protection must come before attending to emotional needs. There are some pitfalls:

1. Being taken advantage of by a "con artist." There are some people around (we are all this way once in a while) who will gladly let you do all of their work. It is not respectful of other persons to do for them what they are capable of doing for themselves because that keeps them weak and inactive, and needlessly dependent on us.

2. Don't get so enthusiastic about helping that you offer more than you can give. It is disrespectful to promise more than you can produce or to attempt something that you can't do, especially if it involves physical condition. Better to refer them to someone who is qualified to help than to bungle the job of helping.

3. Don't give more than you can let go of. Help that is given with strings attached is not servant friendship, but manipulation.

You have skills that other people need. Is it carrying over a bowl of soup or teaching someone to cook, giving a ride or helping someone repair a car, the gift of companionship by playing games with an invalid or baby-sitting for a single parent who otherwise could not have a night out? What are the abilities that you have to share, and who can use them?

There is a great advantage in group decisions in this area so that help is given to persons who need it the most, and given in a way that dignifies them. Acts of mercy are done as our response to Christ's love, not to foster the love of persons whom we have helped.

Request for information. This is similar to the request for physical help in that the other person is asking for something, in this case, information. Again, it may be direct, as "How many chairs should we set up for the banquet?" Or, indirect, "I don't know how many chairs to set up."

When a person needs information, under most circumstances we should give it. Watch for these pitfalls:

1. The "Solomon trip" in which we pretend to be wise when we are not. The only thing worse than an expert is someone who thinks he is.

2. Giving information too soon. Be sure they need it. Be sure they want it. Be sure you have it!

3. Giving cheap advice. The biggest risk in giving quick answers is that we look foolish. Maybe that doesn't matter, for it has been said that advice never hurt anyone—neither the person who gives it nor the person who doesn't take it.

If we are going to give information it should be done in a way that affirms rather than belittles the other person. This is God's style in teaching us. "If any of you lacks wisdom, he should ask God, who gives generously to all without finding fault, and it will be given to him" (Jas. 1:5). God's style—generous and without finding fault—should be our model.

Be brief, but clear. Repeat for emphasis, but don't overdo it. Avoid talking down to the person. If you don't know, admit it, because faking it would be both morally wrong in itself and insulting to the other person. We should avoid being dogmatic. God's laws are perfect; our understanding is not. To ask the question, "What have you thought of already?" shows that we recognize that they have a mind too, and helps them stay involved in the problem-solving process.

Listen for "messages within messages." Along with the need for information there is usually a need and desire for understanding and emotional involvement.

Request for understanding/involvement. Here the need may not be very great, requiring nothing beyond a few minutes of listening. Or, the person may be confused and overwhelmed with numerous problems and uncertainties. Here the basic need cannot be met with a simple answer or helping hand—the person needs companionship or reassurance of personal worth and is asking that you become part of his life, at least for a time.

For example, "I like it here in the retirement home, but the hours do pass rather slowly." Or, "Yeah, things are fine. Mostly, that is." Or, "People here are really different than I'm used to."

We all need understanding and involvement. You can't tell from external circumstances who has a deficit and who doesn't. Listen for the clues they give you.

Again, there is likely to be an indirect approach. A person says, "All my friends are gone. Some moved, some died." That *may* be a way of saying, "I'm lonely. Will you be my friend?" Another person says, "Life sure is complicated these days, isn't it?" This *may* mean, "My life is complicated. I'm confused. Can you help me figure some things out?"

CAUTION: The last thing I want you to do is to try to be a psychological detective. Don't look for an emotional crisis lurking behind *every* simple remark. But, hidden within *some* conversations will be statements that can lead you to great opportunities for service. Just try to see those *when they are there.*

The best first response to the request for understanding/involvement is listening. Then, if appropriate, you can develop a relationship of servant friendship. If not, perhaps you serve the person by helping find other persons who can meet needs you can't meet.

Inappropriate interaction. There are several kinds of conversations that can be very hurtful to the person talking, to persons not present, or to a group. The Bible reader cannot help noticing how clear-cut is God's condemnation of rage, resentment, slander, malice, quarreling, judging, bitterness, filthy language, lying, and chronic complaining. Other inappropriate behavior would include things that are illegal or immoral, seeking to be overly dependent, sarcastic or derogatory humor, asking for participation in activities of questionable judgment, or suggesting anything that could be damaging physically or emotionally to another person.

The best response is usually one in which we *politely decline to take part.* That means that we do more than just remain silent; we do not condone the inappropriate activity. That may seem awkward because there are differences of opinion about what is inappropriate. We suggest this approach because of the harm that may come to persons if inappropriate behavior continues. Silence, likely to be taken as approval, is often not enough.

At the same time we want to show warmth and support for the person in spite of the inappropriate interaction. The style of your response is as important as the content. Put "decline" into your first statement. Remove the condemnation from your vocal style, speaking in an unemotional, even voice. Put "politely" into your second remark—change the subject yourself or ask them to talk about something else. Now put warmth and enthusiasm into your style and listen intently as they talk appropriately.

Here are some examples of inappropriate interaction: "It has really been a shock to be on the finance committee at church. You find out that some of the people with the most money and who really try to control things in the church give practically nothing! Would you believe . . ."

A response that follows our "politely decline to take part in it" rule might be, "I guess you see a serious problem there, but the details wouldn't be important to me." Or, "If it's information about people's giving, that is not for my ears to hear. I'd be glad to talk about a different aspect of the topic—how we as a congregation might learn more about the principles of stewardship."

Two-year-old son says, "Tie my shoe, Daddy." That's appropriate dependency and a good response would be, "Sure!" Sixteen-year-old son says, "Dad, I got my shoe laces knotted up. Would you untangle them for me?" That's over-dependence. A reasonable response would be, "I think that's something you can do for yourself." It's not right to do things for people they are capable of doing for themselves.

A neighbor says, "I just heard a great joke. It's pretty vulgar, but it's funny! It's about . . ." Response: "That sounds like one I probably don't need to hear. Instead, would you give me your opinion about some shrubs I'm thinking about putting in along the driveway?"

There you have it—the risk of embarrassing the other person, which is the dilemma we're faced with every time in responding to something that, to us at least, is inappropriate. We try to keep his embarrassment to a minimum by showing that we care about him as a person; the rest of the risk he will have to accept. We cannot justify letting inappropriate interaction continue because it is destructive. Generally speaking, Christians have been very sloppy in this area of life during recent years. Let's change our little corner of it.

The expression of anger. The other person expresses angry feelings, perhaps directed toward you but more likely directed toward other persons or events. There is a particular style that is preferred when responding to anger.

Anger is usually a symptom of a problem, not the basic problem. If we want to help the angry person get lasting improvement we need to help him talk and then listen carefully so we can help identify the causes of the anger.

The best point at which to begin with an angry person is to assure him that you are willing to listen. This assurance is very likely to have a calming effect that will help the angry person get over the physiological activation that is part of feeling angry.

Keep your words clear and simple. Get the message across that you will listen. Your nonverbal style should be low-key: soft and slow voice, calm body movements, relaxed but attentive posture, and distance a bit more than arm's length.

This is more likely to help anger flow away than any other pattern. Then you can show your willingness to be understanding and involved if that seems appropriate.

Unfortunately, we may react to the anger rather than try to understand the underlying causes. We push the other person away by saying something like, "Let's talk about it when you feel better. We can't do anything worthwhile, while you are this upset." This is a little bit of rejection, something the other person doesn't need and that will probably just lead to his feeling angrier.

We might ignore it by changing the subject or walking away, again rejecting and giving more frustration. We may tell the other person how to act, "Oh, that's no big deal. You shouldn't get upset." We might try to give a rational explanation why he shouldn't be angry but the angry person is unlikely to benefit from those good explanations because the flow of anger pushes away the inward flow of reason. Even if he heard your reasons it may not be all that you would want to do because of the importance of getting into the underlying conditions.

Now we have considered two processes that usually happen in the early seconds in an encounter with another person: (1) contact behaviors through which we show whether or not we wish to interact, and (2) assessment, a system by which we can sort out what we think the other person wants or needs. We also looked at some of the "dos and don'ts" of various response styles. Now we'll look at two more relational skills that are important in servant friendship.

Remembering Names

I have often asked seminar groups, "How many of you are the world's worst at remembering names?" About two-thirds of the people in a group will lay claim to this title, apparently the world's most coveted championship! Most people don't do well, but *you* can—and easily—if you want to.

There are four simple steps.

1. Hear it. It's amazing how we can criticize ourselves for not remembering something we never heard. The problem is two-fold. When we meet someone new we are likely to be thinking things such as: "What will he think of me? Is my breath okay? What am I going to say?" and so on. That interferes with hearing the other person. Also, and probably more important, people often are careless in giving their own name, rattling it off with a quick mumble so that we don't have a chance in the first place.

Easy to fix that problem: if you don't hear it, ask him to repeat it. Asking a person to repeat his or her name, or to spell it, is a compliment that says, "You are important enough to me that I want to know your name."

2. After you hear the name, use it. This reinforces it in your mind as you use it and hear yourself using it. And if you haven't gotten it right you can be corrected. Work the name into such phrases as, "It is really nice to meet you, Alice," or "How long have you lived in Phoenix, Ken?"

3. See it. There are two ways—in your mind and on paper. Many persons have the knack, especially with a little practice, of seeing the image of the name in their mind. This can be in big, bold letters for a big, bold person, or in fancy script for another or in flashing lights like a movie marquee, or whatever fits. It can be superimposed

by the face as you see on television. Or, when you can, make a list of new names to remember and review that from time to time. Seeing the name uses the perceptual channel of vision in addition to the channel of hearing that you started with.

If you use these three steps you'll be far better than almost everyone else. If you want to be sensational, add one more method.

4. Connect the name with other information about the person. This method takes more practice than the others and is not necessary unless you are learning many names within a short period of time.

Get a mental image that connects the name with something else. For example, the name "Rich Walters." Picture the wall of a bank vault with piles of money heaped up against it, a *rich wall.* But the wall is sad—tears are actually flowing from it: *rich wall tears.* Corny? Yes, but effective. You never had that image in your mind before. It's different, so it will stick. Now put me in there—add the image of a lanky, brown-haired guy lounging on the floor with his back against the money. Leave the tears on the wall, put only a smile on my face. It's locked in your memory now. There is an image to connect with every name and with practice you will be able to invent them quickly.

Giving and Receiving Compliments

If you're like most Christians, you give compliments with reasonable skill, but in receiving them—well, it's probably something like this: A compliment is given, "Oh, there you are. Glad I saw you because I wanted to say something about how well you did in leading the meeting Wednesday. You did a super job!"

And the response, "Are you kidding? I was never so embarrassed. I was so disorganized; left some of my papers at home so I was fumbling along. Left out two important points entirely. I'm really ashamed!"

That kind of response has about the same effect as saying, "If you knew how to judge a meeting you wouldn't say such stupid things." Without intending to, it not only rejects the compliment but returns for it an insult.

Why? Most often, false modesty—fear of pride; fear of appearing proud. There are several other reasons why people deny deserved compliments: they have had so many phony compliments that they don't trust any now; in accepting a compliment they are agreeing to a level of performance that creates a standard to live up to in the future; and persons with low self-esteem simply feel that they do not deserve it.

You probably deserve all the compliments you can get so accept them—graciously. Simply say, "Thank you." If you want variety, tell how the compliment makes you feel as, "That's nice to hear," or "I appreciate your saying that," or "You've really made my day by saying that. Thanks!"

Don't think that accepting a few compliments will turn you into a self-centered snob. You won't get that many anyway—compliments are in short supply. Accept them, and give them, especially to the people who are reluctant to accept them and who probably need them the most.

Discussion Questions

1. Give your feelings about the "contact phase" of a new relationship. Is it painful or is it enjoyable for you? For others?
2. How important do you think awareness of the nonverbal contact behaviors is? Relate an experience you've had when ineffective nonverbal contact behaviors were glaringly noticeable.
3. When does giving help to a person leave the category of servant friendship and turn into manipulation?

Chapter Seven

Improve Your Listening Skills

Haley was a pushover. Everyone in the shop knew that even though Haley hated tobacco smoke he'd still loan a guy cigarette money and say, "My pleasure." You could borrow anything from him and he'd say, "My pleasure." He was such a soft touch it got to be a joke. He was referred to as "My Pleasure Haley" and there were wisecracks, but he didn't lose respect for it. It was the same way at home, in the neighborhood, and everywhere else I guess, until the time the old stranger showed up at church.

It was a Thursday in the summer, during Haley's vacation, and he had gone down to the church to fix some things. Haley and the pastor were checking the signboard on the front lawn when they saw the old man approaching.

"A tramp!" Haley said with awe in his voice. "An old-timey tramp! I haven't seen one of them in years. The last of a vanishing breed."

The pastor said dryly, "You'd not say that if you were here every day."

The old man moved shyly toward them and eyes looking in the general direction of the VISITORS WEL-

COME phrase said, "Could you help an unfortunate?" His wizened skin, the sallow gray of a skid-row sidewalk, hung loosely from his face, joyless as a weather-beaten grave wreath. A navy blue topcoat, his bed and blanket, was on his back. His hair, with not so much gray as was in his face, had been neatly cut perhaps a month ago.

"Where have you come from?" the fascinated Haley asked.

"Wales," he said flatly. "Wales. Came over in 1917."

"And since then?"

"From Williamsport today. Want to get down to Altoona. There's a Salvation Army place there."

He noticed Haley's eyes on the duffle bag. "A Methodist minister gave me that. United Methodist minister down in West Virginia. Yes, sir. He had that in Europe with him in the war, he said, and he gave it to me. He saw my bag wasn't any good and he gave me this." His eyes remained toward the ground; his manner was hopeful, expectant.

The minister shifted from foot to foot, his eyes trying to catch Haley's. "Well, you have a good day for traveling, sir. You're on the Altoona Pike now. Just follow this out of town the way you're going. With any luck at all you'll make it well before dark. Don't you think so, Haley?"

Haley jumped. "What? . . . Uh, what?"

"He could make it to Altoona by dark, don't you think? With any luck at all getting rides. Don't you think?"

"Oh, I'm not so sure," Haley responded slowly. "Might rain, too. You know, Pastor, how Rose and me love company. He could stay over and then in the morning we can talk about finding a more permanent place for him to stay . . . I mean," he turned to the old man, "for you to stay. That is, if you want to . . . if you like it here. For a while, anyway. If you want to."

The minister looked intently at the steeple, the old man shifted from foot to foot, and The Plan swept forward in Haley's mind.

"If you want to," Haley went on, "we'd love to have you stay over. We do that a lot—put people up. It's our pleasure, me and Rose. Her kin came from Wales, even. And, look, we've got everything here they've got in Altoona. Food, sleep, jobs and everything. You name it, we've got it. Stay with me and Rose tonight and see if you don't like it." His voice was tinged with pleading.

The old man said, "Well . . ."

"Then it's settled," Haley said.

Haley reached out to carry the duffle bag but the old man pulled it close. "It's no trouble. I'm used to it. You're a kind man to take pity on a poor unfortunate like myself. You're a kind man."

That evening, after a meatloaf dinner, Haley, Rose and their guest sat around the kitchen table. Haley cleared his throat and said, "Uh, funny thing, but, uh, we don't know your name."

"Robinson."

"Fine name, Robinson. Mine's Haley. Ernest Haley."

"Mind if I have a short smoke, Mr. Haley?"

"Go right ahead; go right ahead."

Robinson pulled out cigarette paper and a tin of tobacco and Haley quickly said, "Look, if you want the other kind we'll go get 'em."

"It's no trouble. I'm used to it. But you're a kind man."

At the end of his smoke he rubbed it out on the saucer Rose had set out and carefully recycled the unsmoked shreds back to the Prince Albert can.

Finally Haley could take his new friend down to his shop in the basement. He opened every drawer and box showing off the tools and gadgets. Robinson was pretty quiet but, to Haley's delight, seemed to be familiar with everything. He even recognized the set of screw extractors and when Haley saw him pick up a micrometer he thought, "Why, those tools lay in his hand like he's used them all his life," and smiled proudly.

Later the three of them sat around the table with coffee, Haley firing questions and Robinson obliging with sparse answers. When Haley found out that Robinson had been a tool-and-die maker he was ecstatic. It fit The Plan with precision, but he couldn't say anything yet—best not to get an old man's hopes up.

At bedtime Haley felt the same as he had December 24, age nine. The Plan, each cog and bearing fitting perfectly together, revolved in his mind for hours but he woke early with a sense of excitement.

While he shaved, The Plan was jaunty on his mind. He peeked in on Robinson and was pleased to see him sleeping yet, then told Rose, "I'm too busy for breakfast—things to do and people to see. Fix it for the two of you and I'll be back at 10:30. With good news!"

He was back on time, good news bursting from his face—stunned cold when Rose told him the old man had gone.

"Gone? . . . Gone? That can't be." He sat down at the kitchen table, staring at the gray ash-smudge on the saucer. "That just can't be. What did he say?"

"He said, 'Thank you, ma'am, but I best be going. Want to get down to Altoona. You're a kind lady, to do what you've done. Thank you again, ma'am.' "

"That's it?"

"That's it."

"That's all?"

"All of it."

"Nothing about me?"

"Best as I can remember, that's all he said."

Haley jumped to his feet. "Of all the dirty tricks! After all I've done for him! No gratitude, no ambition, no self-respect! You just can't trust anybody anymore!"

He sat down again, pulled the saucer close, and gripped it with both hands. "Well, maybe everybody wants a handout these days but they aren't going to get it from me.

I'd be a fool to bust my back helping another person again."

And he never did.

Talking: toy of the foolish;
   Listening: joy of the wise.
Talking: learned too early;
   Listening: learned too late.
Talking: demanding, commanding, preempting, droning,
     growling, brawling, bawling, pushy, shoving noise;
   Listening: affirming, nourishing, renewing cool water.
Talking: fakeable;
   Listening: authentic, or non-existent.
Talking, unless listened to, has no more influence than its
   last echo;
   Listening, when given with integrity, creates influence.
Listening: the big half of communication, the difficult half.
Listening: with ears to hear the words,
    with eyes to receive nonverbal signals of act and mood
     too awesome or too delicate to put into words,
    with mind to process for knowledge,
    with the help of the Holy Spirit in discerning so that
     knowledge is understood and used wisely,
    with wholeness which communicates attitudes as we
     listen,
    with energy and sensitivity, with concern and accept-
     ance.
Listening: the quiet gift, the silence that speaks "I care."

Robinson listened. It made a difference to him, as it does for us—every time.

Listening is usually the most important first response when the need is for understanding/involvement. Let us consider the essential elements of listening so that we may be better servant friends.

Listening with Ears

Ears are what we think of first in connection with listening and they're important, sure, though no more important than the other matters described in this chapter. We use our ears to hear the words of another person—to gather the information that will help us understand them.

The first step in using your ears well is to not use your mouth at the same time. Your ears don't work when your mouth is running. This concept leads to Rule One: Shut up. Give yourself a chance to hear.

For another person to talk against the competition of your talking is like spitting against the wind, and most people aren't foolish enough to do it. This leads to Rule Two: Shut up. Give them a chance to talk.

Other persons will feel more free to talk if you invite (not demand) them to talk. This leads to Rule Three: If you can't shut up, invite them to talk. Then shut up. Make it easy for others to talk.

Listening with Eyes

The process of communicating to another person involves sending and receiving messages about content and feelings. In our culture we emphasize content—objects, places, concepts, events, people—much more than talking about our feelings—how these content things affect us. Men, especially, give more attention to content.

To know a person well enough to be a servant friend requires understanding feelings, which are communicated primarily nonverbally—without the use of words. Nonverbal channels of communication include gestures, the use of space, posture, eye contact, facial expression, loudness or softness of voice, tone of voice, level of energy, even style of dress or carefulness of grooming, and many more. There are as many options in nonverbal styles as there are in choice of words.

When it comes to communicating feelings, the nonverbal methods are far more important than the verbal. Facial expression and tone of voice are particularly important in the communication of feelings. Careful scientific studies show that if we pay attention only to the words we probably will not accurately understand how another person feels.

It is useful for us to try to pick up—by watching and listening closely—as much of what the other person is telling us as possible. Watch for facial expression. Listen for tone of voice as well as the words. If it is appropriate for you to touch, notice the other person's level of muscle tension.

Table number 1 suggests how a lot of people often show several basic feelings. But, there are many, many variations in nonverbal communication—people are different from each other. The same person is different from time to time and cultures are different from one place to another.

Use these suggestions as general guidelines to help you increase your awareness of nonverbal behaviors. Use these signals as hunches—as clues—to how a person *may* feel. Be cautious! When you notice a nonverbal behavior and you think it means something, look for other signs that agree or disagree with what you saw first. Do not play amateur analyst. *Do not jump to conclusions!*

Awareness of nonverbal clues such as these can help us understand other persons more completely and thereby be more effective as servant friends. One way to use a hunch about another's feelings is to comment or inquire on the basis of what you have noticed. "You seem a little jittery today. Anything wrong?" Or, "You're not talking as much as usual today." Or, "I'm not sure what it is, but you don't seem quite like yourself today."

As we pay more attention to other persons, we learn more about ourselves as well. We can learn what effect we have on people, which can help us make fewer human relations mistakes.

Listening with the Mind

The bugaboo in communication is misunderstanding. It happens inevitably because words have many different meanings. Even the word "word" has 23 definitions in my ordinary little dictionary. That makes problems.

When I speak to you I think I know what I mean. What I say is not quite what I think. You hear part of what I say. You understand part of what you hear. After my thought has gone through three minor distortions you may understand it as something quite different than I intended. No one is at fault—this is only part of being a human being.

One of the things we can do to keep misunderstanding at a minimum is to check back frequently with the talker to see if we are understanding what he or she intends. A good way to do that is occasionally to summarize and paraphrase what the talker has just said. This method is often called "active listening." It is a very powerful relational tool when used well and used appropriately. As the case with any tool, it can seem ridiculous when used at the wrong time. And in some training programs active listening has been presented as though it were the only communication skill to use. Not so!

We will not teach the skill of active listening in this book because, being a skill, it is best taught in a coaching process in which the mistakes made during practice can be corrected. But a summary is in order.

Active listening is the method used in non-directive counseling. Counseling that is totally non-directive is based on the assumption that man is essentially good and, given a relationship of warm, respectful support, will come to the right conclusions in life decisions and motivate self to take the right action. This recognizes that there is a lot about mankind that is capable and good, but ignores the

*NONVERBAL COMMUNICATION

	DEPRESSION	ANXIETY
	often shows in:	often shows in:
head	down	stiff movement; chin down
face	frown	flushed; pale
mouth	downturned; tightness	tightness; clenching teeth
eye contact	little or none	darting glances; vigilant
hands	rubbing; clutching	tightness; gripping; sweaty palms
posture	hunches while sitting	frequent movement; crouching; hunches shoulders
position	moves away	angled away; protective
distance	more than usual	moderately away
energy	low	may be high
general	lack of interest; avoids people or activities	jerky movements; tics; guards "territory"

	ANGER	LOW SELF-WORTH
	often shows in:	often shows in:
head	forward or tilted upward	downward
face	angry frown (eyebrows down at center)	half-smiles; quickly follows your expressions
mouth	lips tensed; pushed forward	quivering; halting speech
eye contact	excessive; defiant	low; peeking
hands	clenching; fist; thumping (symbolic hitting)	restless
posture	edge of chair	way back as if to be invisible, or on edge as if to run; protective
distance	moves into others' space	more than usual or, if they trust you, extra close
energy	high	low
general	acting out such as slamming door, jerking or shoving objects, extra noisy	always watching for signs of approval or disapproval from others

*Hundreds of pieces of literature in scientific journals were consulted in the preparation of these lists. They appear in more detailed form in "Nonverbal Communication in Group Counseling" by R. P. Walters, a chapter in *Group Counseling: A Developmental Approach* (2nd ed.) by G. M. Gazda. Boston: Allyn and Bacon, 1978.

Table 1

other side of man's condition—an attraction to evil because of inherent sin.

The active listening process itself is an expression of the Christian principle of "Rejoice with those who rejoice; mourn with those who mourn" (Rom. 12:15). It allows the talker to set the direction and pace of the conversation. The more comfortable the talker is, the more information you get, which increases your potential for service. That promotes self-understanding by the talker. Many people really do solve their own problems when given a chance to "think out loud" in the presence of a caring person.

Active listening communicates respect because you are not inflicting Verbal Villains on the talker. It is more difficult to do than the Verbal Villains, something the talker will sense and recognize as your gift of caring.

Following is a brief excerpt of an active listening conversation. This is between Rob, who has a problem, and Al, who uses active listening.

Rob: Well, Friday at last! I thought the weekend would never come.

Al: Sounds like it's been a long week for you.

Rob: Probably the longest week of my life.

Al: Must have really been rough!

Rob: You wouldn't believe it. If it wasn't one thing, it was another. I couldn't win for losing.

Al: Sounds overwhelming. I guess you felt kind of trapped.

Rob: Trapped is right! Trapped under a 90-thousand-ton boulder.

Al: With these things going on, Rob, it must really be difficult for you to know what to do about it.

Up to this point all of Al's responses have been in the active listening style. He continues speaking, only now, rather than using active listening, he is offering his help.

Al: I don't know if this is anything that you want to talk
with me about, or if there is anything I can do to
help, but if I can I'd sure like to have a chance to
try.

Rob: Yeah, I'd like to talk. It isn't easy to talk about this
stuff, but . . . well, do you know where I could get
some help in filing for bankruptcy?

Now, in addition to the need for understanding/in-
volvement, Rob has asked a specific question. Al will
answer that, but along with giving the information to the
question will continue to offer his understanding/involve-
ment. He wouldn't suddenly limit his conversation to a
lesson in business law.

The scenario above illustrates active listening but also
shows how it fits in as only one of several communication
styles. The non-directive process is valuable, especially in
helping persons get all the pieces of the puzzle out on the
table so that they can be worked on, but the highly direc-
tive processes such as confrontation are equally important
in servant friendship.

Listening with Wholeness

You never stop communicating. Even as you listen,
your body communicates your attitudes, giving the talker
an impression of whether or not you are listening, are
interested, and how you feel about him or her as a person.
These impressions may or may not be accurate, but they
have a powerful effect on the talker.

Few persons are willing to talk about important things
when it seems to them that they are not being listened to.
So, it is important that you not only listen, but that your
nonverbal behaviors show that you are. We call the behaviors used by the listener "attending skills."

Table 2 shows behaviors that are likely to be ineffective and those that are likely to be effective. There is room

for a lot of individual variation within these guidelines; they are not absolute, specific rules.

Effective attending skills are comfortable to use and help you listen and remember. They show your interest in and respect for the talker. They work only if you have genuine interest and respect—if you are trying to be manipulative your true feelings will leak out and be noticed.

Most persons can make improvement more quickly in communication with others by improving attending skills than by any other one part of the process. How effective are your attending skills now?

Listening with God's Help

One reason, a sufficient reason, that listening is important is because God commands it. His Word makes it clear that it is important to listen to Him: "Give ear and come to me; hear me, that your soul may live" (Isa. 55:3); to listen to the authority of Scripture, "Let the wise listen and add to their learning, and let the discerning get guidance" (Prov. 1:5); and to listen to one another, "Everyone should be quick to listen, slow to speak" (Jas. 1:19).

Listening is not an end in itself, of course, but a guide to our actions. "Do not merely listen to the word, and so deceive yourselves. Do what it says" (Jas. 1:22).

God wants us to work on behalf of the people around us. But He doesn't give us jobs to do without making available to us the resources to accomplish them. "For it is God who is at work within you, giving you the will and the power to achieve his purpose" (Phil. 2:13, *Phillips*).

James talks of "wisdom that comes from heaven" (Jas. 3:17) and goes on to urge the reader to seek the Lord as the only way of finding true wisdom. Peter points out (see 2 Pet. 3:15-18) that Paul's wisdom was a gift from God and that we, too, grow in grace by seeking God. We know the truth by coming to know God, as we can through Christ (see John 8:31,32).

Paul prayed on behalf of the Ephesians that God would give them the spirit of wisdom and revelation, so that they might know Him better (see Eph. 1:17). We certainly can know God, as He promised the exiled children of Israel, "You will call upon me and come and pray to me, and I will listen to you. You will seek me and find me when you seek me with all your heart" (Jer. 29:12,13). Not only do we meet God, but He faithfully is with us no matter what happens. "I will be with you" (Isa. 43:2). He is with us in His Word, through teaching and fellowship of a community of believers, and in the Holy Spirit. "In the same way, the Spirit helps us in our weakness" (Rom. 8:26).

Some Christians will be given special gifts of wisdom and discernment. Each of us will be given the wisdom that we will need for the tasks to which we have been called.

Earlier in the book we noted, for a different reason, James 1:5, "If any of you lacks wisdom, he should ask God, who gives generously to all without finding fault, and it will be given to him." This is a very important verse to me personally because I often am aware that I lack wisdom. God has proved to me on many occasions that He does give generously—as we need, and as we ask.

Hebrews closes with a benediction that includes the words, "May the God of peace . . . equip you with everything good for doing his will" (vv. 20,21). It is an appropriate prayer for us to use on our own behalf.

We're all more alike than we are different. Find and nurture the areas of common interest. Help the person, even (or especially?) an enemy: "Give him food to eat . . . water to drink. In doing this, you will heap burning coals on his head, and the Lord will reward you" (Prov. 25:21,22).

Pray that you will be yielded fully to the Lord, in which case the Spirit will develop in you love, joy, peace, patience, kindness, goodness, faithfulness, gentleness and

Attending Skills

INEFFECTIVE USE	NONVERBAL MODES OF COMMUNICATION	EFFECTIVE USE
Doing any of these things will probably close off or slow down the conversation		These behaviors encourage talk because they show acceptance and respect for the other person.
spread among activities	Attention	given fully to talker
distant; very close	Space	approximate arm's length
away	Movement	toward
slouching; rigid; seated leaning away	Posture	relaxed, but attentive; seated leaning slightly toward
absent; defiant; jittery	Eye contact	regular
slow to notice talker; in a hurry	Time	respond at first opportunity; share time with them
used to keep distance between persons	Feet and legs (in sitting)	unobtrusive
used as a barrier	Furniture	used to draw persons together
does not match feelings; scowl; blank look	Facial expression	matches your own or other's feelings; smile
compete for attention with your words	Gestures	highlight your words; unobtrusive; smooth
obvious; distracting	Mannerisms	none, or unobtrusive
very loud or very soft	Voice: volume	clearly audible
impatient or staccato; very slow or hesitant	Voice: rate	average, or a bit slower
apathetic; sleepy; jumpy; pushy	Energy level	alert; stays alert throughout a long conversation
sloppy; garish; provocative	Dress; grooming	tasteful

Table 2

self-control (see Gal. 5:22,23). And your friends won't recognize you.

Listening with Acceptance

Each person is worthwhile simply because he or she exists, is made in God's image. Nothing can add to that as a basis for worth; nothing can take it away.

In our relationships Christ commands, "Love one another. As I have loved you, so you must love one another" (John 13:34).

Love is expressed by first accepting the other as a person with worth, and communicating that acceptance. We cannot accept or condone behavior that is wrong and we should not pretend to. But if we want to help a person change wrong behavior we must first accept and love him or her as a person, and communicate that through what we say and do.

We can celebrate the person's appropriate actions and affirm his potential for more worthwhile behavior. This can be done even as we are unable to accept certain past, present, or planned behavior.

Don't pry into unworthwhile past behavior. If it is forgiven, it is no longer an issue with God and need not be with us; if it is not forgiven, teach about forgiveness. The details of past events should not matter to you.

Seek to understand what forces have shaped the other person's life view. This can help you avoid overreacting to offensive behavior and still accept the person.

Listening is a door into the other person's life; through listening you learn of fears, joys, sorrows and aspirations that motivate or inhibit that person. Giving the gift of listening is a powerful way of proving that you care and can be trusted. Listen well, and move on to earn and nurture trust in the friendship.

Discussion Questions

1. What flaw or flaws do you see in Haley's character? Do you know anyone like him? In what ways are you like Haley?
2. If nonverbal clues are so important in accurately understanding how a person feels, how do you account for the fact that we so often overlook them? What can we do about this?
3. What are some things we can do to aid in understanding a person better, or to keep misunderstanding at a minimum?
4. Describe the ways in which active listening is an expression of the principle, "Rejoice with those who rejoice; mourn with those who mourn" (Rom. 12:15).
5. Discuss the importance of attending skills in the light of what you have experienced in this area—with both ineffective use and effective use. Give examples.
6. Can you share an experience in which you misinterpreted the nonverbal behavior of another person?
7. What did Robinson want? What did he need? What did Haley want? What did Haley offer?
8. Speculate about what may have motivated Haley's generosity in the past. How do you suppose he may have felt on those occasions? What is the proper basis for generosity? What is the first step in helping others?

Chapter Eight

Proving I Care: Trust

Ernest Haley was comfortable, exquisitely so, horizontal in his recliner before the television, taking dead aim through his feet like gun sights.

Rose appeared at the door behind him, peering in timidly. Her timing was perfect—not only during a commercial, but between games! She moved behind the chair.

"I wish you could have been there. Such a spirit of enthusiasm and cooperation. Everyone was of the same mind! It was wonderful!"

"Sure, sure. The men weren't there." He didn't move. "It's easy enough for the women to figure out how to spend more of our money."

"Lots of men were there. Most of them."

"Well, I still say it's stupid! And it isn't even right to call a church meeting on a Sunday afternoon in the middle of football season!"

"There are some things more important than football, and helping the refugees of the world is one of them!"

"Sure, everyone wants me to feed 'em! I can't do it, and I won't!" His angry eyes fired straight ahead.

"Ernest. . . ." She knelt beside the chair and rubbed his arm, slowly kneading the tension away. "Ernest, you've been so different the last few months. You're just not cheerful like you've always been."

"I've learned some things about life."

"What do you mean?"

"You can't trust people. They only want to take advantage of you."

"Well . . . what? Why—why do you say that?"

"You remember what happened three months ago?"

"You mean that nice Mr. Robinson?"

"No. I mean that phony Robinson the bum, the guy who refused to work for a living!"

His arm jerked in her hands; it felt like stone. She fumbled for words. "That was three months ago. And it was different—quite different."

"Animal crackers!"

Rose felt tears in her eyes. She couldn't have spoken if she had known what to say.

"You can't trust people," he went on. "Any of 'em. Or God either, for all I know!"

Haley's arm dropped from her hands—limp, almost lifeless. He closed his eyes and turned slightly away. She thought, though she wasn't sure, she had seen tears in his eyes.

A month went past and they had not discussed the resettlement project. Haley knew, from reports at church, that the Asian family the church was sponsoring was arriving. A reception was being held that evening.

"Ernest, I wish you'd change your mind and go. It's at the Mills's home. You always enjoy them."

"The Cowboys and the Rams are playing. Hasn't the committee heard of Monday night football?"

Rose said nothing, though her husband saw the lonely ache in her eyes.

"I'd be out of half the conversation at the shop if I didn't keep up with football."

"Enjoy the game." She kissed him good-bye.

When she returned, Haley was seated at the dinette, both elbows on the table. He held a coffee cup with both hands, sipping cautiously. When Rose entered he set the coffee down but did not turn around.

"I thought you'd never get back."

"It was really nice."

"It wouldn't have been any fun for me."

Rose stood behind him and with both hands massaged his neck and shoulders. She smiled the bittersweet combination of love and frustration. "The men all went downstairs and watched the ball game."

Rose was seated at the dinette. "Thanks for offering to fix lunch. You'll spoil me, waiting on me like this!"

"Grilled cheese and tomato soup isn't much, but it's my pleasure. My pleasure." Haley hummed as he carried the food to the table.

"You know," he said, "that Mr. Tran is really something! Only been in this country six months and talks English like the best of us. Quick, quick mind. And a genius with his hands."

Rose brightened. "The two of you were talking a plenty in the basement this morning. And you both came up smiling."

"Yeah, we hit it off pretty good."

"What was that he had with him?"

"Oh," as he looked intently at his soup, "just a micrometer."

"It was your best one, wasn't it?"

"Yeah."

"The one you've always kept under lock and key?"

"Yeah." He looked at her with a sheepish, but relaxed grin. "Like you say, 'Helping people can be okay.' Trusting them, even, that's what it's all about."

Trusting is placing some of your security into another

person's control. We are forced to trust others hundreds of times a day in order to go about routine living. In the simple act of going out for a Big Mac we trust the driving of others and the care taken over the food by persons who raised the beef, inspected it, kept it refrigerated, prepared it and served it.

Giving trust to others, including a multitude of strangers, is a requirement in many areas of life. We must trust ourselves in those areas, too.

We trust in the realm of financial and corporate systems—that the fire department will come when we need them and that a bank manages our money responsibly. We trust in the informational realm as we read a newspaper or attend school.

We trust in the spiritual and emotional realms. Christians trust that God's Word is true and that He keeps His promises. We trust that a Christian pattern of living is best. We trust spiritual leaders to guide us into truth. We trust others to not ridicule us when we tell how we feel or what we believe. We trust those we love to continue to love us, for if they reject us it will be painful.

Giving trust in the spiritual and emotional areas of life is even more important than giving trust in the other areas if we are to have truly joyous living, but it is optional. In our society it is simpler to survive without friends than to survive without a grocery store. So, many persons give more trust to the stranger at the grocery store than to their neighbors. As a result they survive, but they don't live. Why do they make this choice? Because trust involves risk—putting some of our security into another person's control. Yet we must.

It is only by taking risks that we gain rewards. It is only by trusting God and other persons that we can get our relational needs adequately satisfied.

In addition to trusting others it is also essential that we receive the trust of others. Being trusted increases our sense of identity, our self-confidence, and our self-esteem.

Let's look at six characteristic behaviors of persons who can be trusted and then consider three conditions that must form the foundation for our behavior. With attention to these things you will receive trust because you will have earned it.

1. *If you can trust me, I will not intrude into your life with that which is hurtful to you. I will not steal your time, trample roughly through your tranquility, litter your life with marginal morality, or interrupt your progress with shabby shortcuts.*

Chances are you can't imagine yourself physically attacking and trying to injure another person. You are probably not a burglar. The thought of going to the nearest library and running atop the tables shouting at the top of your voice has probably not occurred to you.

You and I simply do not do the blatant things that are hurtful to others—we are much too law-abiding and polite for that. Or is it timidity that holds us in check?

Consider, though, that we might do other things that, even though quiet and unnoticed, would be just as destructive. Just as a leaky battery can corrode and destroy a flashlight, we can quietly do things that corrode and ultimately destroy the lives of persons around us.

There are many things that fit this category—gossiping, encouraging a friend to spend more than he or she can afford, pressing one to cheat on a diet, frazzling the nerves with chatter about ourselves, leading a person into any kind of activity that is hurtful. That these things are wrong is self-evident so I'll limit detailed attention to one topic: physical intimacy.

A servant friendship is an opportunity to exchange perceptions, opinions and insights, to give understanding, and to be understood. It becomes an emotionally intimate relationship, and a strong love between persons often develops. Along with emotional intimacy and appropriate love for a person may come the desire for physical intimacy.

The desire to touch and to be touched is God given, so it's fine, and we should cultivate and enjoy tactile stimulation—touch—just as we enjoy our senses of sight, hearing, smell, and taste. But, because of the close association with sexual activity, touching persons—especially between sexes—is quite another matter, with hazards that must be pointed out.

"Touching" is an imprecise term. It includes shaking hands and sexual intercourse, and a million in-between behaviors so varied and affected by context and intention that to be more specific is futile. Some things are clear: the Bible prohibits fornication, adultery, and sexual perversions—physical or in the heart. But what about the million in-betweens?

I'm in favor of more freedom to touch others *nonsexually*. Many Christians would be more effective relationally, and more spontaneous personally, if they would express themselves more in giving and receiving touch. But I have grave concerns about the dangers in touching and elaborate on the subject here for three reasons:

First, because the pressure to touch inappropriately is strong. In a couple of decades we have moved from a Victorian heritage which said don't do any touching to a "new morality" (the old immorality) that bombards us with encouragement to do too much.

Second, because the hazards are real and the problems immense. Anyone who thinks immorality isn't a problem among well-intentioned Christian people should consult the statistics.

Third, some widely-read Christian statements have not pointed out the dangers.

Most sexual problems involving Christians begin with behavior that is not only proper but is commendable—

understanding and seeking to help meet the legitimate needs of the other person—being a servant friend. Then the emotional or physical intimacy can cross a border into the area that is definitely sin. We need to know how to avoid sin and pursue righteousness.

Here are some questions that you might ask yourself in regard to touching. These may help you evaluate and control your behavior in "in-between" situations.

(1) How does the other person perceive this? What does he/she think it means? Is my touching misunderstood as a sexual advance by the person being touched or by observers?

(2) Is the other person uncomfortable? There is a great deal of variation in touching behavior among cultures and among persons within a culture. Some persons don't like to be touched, so to touch them would be an intrusion. If the other person draws back from being touched, adjust your behavior accordingly.

(3) Does the touching (or talking about it or thinking about it) subtract from or add to the spirituality of either person?

(4) Am I interested in the person or am I interested in touching the person? Is it for the other person or for me? The guiding principle of servant friendship is unselfish love, and the test of our behavior is if what we say or do is for the benefit of the other person or not. Touching can be beneficial or it can create major problems.

(5) How do, or how would, others perceive this? Will they infer more from a hug than they should and how will that affect their behavior and our influence on them? The same question applies to appearances given by the amount of time we spend isolated with other persons.

When two persons are attracted to each other and must spend a lot of time together—on a job, for example—they might benefit by talking explicitly about the sexual attraction they feel, the potential dilemmas they face, and what they will do. One option is to dedicate the friendship to the Lord's use. To pray together, such as: "Lord, we thank you for this friendship, for the joy of knowing each other, for the fun we have together, and for the things that we learn from each other. Help us to not spoil this friendship in any way. Protect us from the expression of any of our human impulses that would not be pleasing to you. Instead, show us how we may return to your service the benefits that we gain from this friendship. Amen."

It seems popular to rationalize in this area and one line goes, "This is beyond my control. I didn't know what was happening." I don't buy that. Touching is one among many kinds of physical pleasures. We can tell them apart. We can distinguish the pleasure of tasting a juicy steak from the pleasure of hearing favorite music from the pleasure of a warm tub bath. We can also distinguish the pleasure of touch that is sexual from that which is not. Since we can tell the difference we are responsible to God and to other persons to appropriately control our behavior.

Another rationalization goes, "I have physical needs and they have to be met." That's true, but it doesn't apply here; fornication, adultery, and sexual perversions are not physical needs, they are sins.

And another one goes, "It isn't fair for God to let me be tempted in this way. I told God it would be okay for me to be tempted to shave my head or to take bassoon lessons, to be tempted to dress in a Santa Claus suit in July or to climb Pike's Peak on my hands and knees, but why doesn't He do something about these temptations that are so appealing?" He has, of course: God promises that we will never be tempted at an intensity greater than we can resist. (See 1 Cor. 10:13.)

The responsibility is back to us. But if we share it with the Lord, getting along in this area is not that tough.

2. If you can trust me, I will not compete for your attention with that in your life which is more important for you. I will not divert you from devotion to God, from proper attention to career, from companionship with family.

College was easy for Dean. He could do his school-work, keep a part-time job, be active socially, and still have lots of time left over to goof off. So he was frequently saying to his roommate, "Let's play a little Ping-Pong" or "It's a great day for tennis" or "There's a great game on the tube. Bring your books down to the lounge and let's watch it." At the end of the year Dean had nearly a straight-A average; his roommate was on academic proba-tion.

Whose fault? The roommate was failing academically because he failed personally—he had not disciplined him-self and had not asserted himself against Dean's distrac-tions. But Dean was responsible too—he failed his room-mate as a friend by urging the distractions.

Harold was the concerned teacher of an adult Bible course. Sandy was spiritually hungry and lonely. They spent much time together in addition to the classes. Harold tutored her about the Bible and listened to her family problems. He cared, and she loved it. She talked about Harold so much to her husband that he quit going to church. Harold was physically proper, but invaded Sandy's life with emotional adultery by distracting her from her primary relationship, her marriage.

Carl, a successful attorney, spoke with anguish as he said, "It's a bind! The partnership wants me to produce more and I want to because I enjoy my work. My church asks me to help out and I know that's important, too. And I want my family to be the most important part of my life. But I get spread so thin I'm not doing anything right. It really frustrates me!"

Sound familiar? All persons of competence face the

problem of excessive demands being made on their time.

When we are in leadership at work, church, or home, do we do that to people? We should not chip away at another person's capacity to take care of his or her obligations.

It especially distresses me when, in the counseling office, I meet pastors or their family members upon whom the congregation has made such extreme demands that personal and family needs have been neglected. All pastors should recognize this hazard, and I think most of them do; all parishioners should see to it that the pastor's personal and family time is protected, and few do that. When we are in administrative relationship with another—as a parishioner is with a pastor—we have a trust responsibility to help that person fulfill his/her priorities.

3. If you can trust me, I will not keep from you the truth you need to learn in order to become more whole. If it will help you, I will lovingly confront you with your failure to use your strengths, with your weaknesses, or with your inconsistencies with God's truth.

Nothing destroys trust faster than keeping secrets, yet it can be very difficult to tell other people something that they don't want to hear, no matter how valuable it might be for them to hear it. Doing that is confrontation, which we cover in chapter 10.

Part of the truth that we need to share with other people is praise. Give honest praise in a simple and direct way, and only when it is deserved. If you say to someone, "You look terrific!" and actually her hair is a mess and her clothes are dirty and wrinkled, she will know you are being phony—the opposite of being a trustworthy person.

We are to witness, and we do—constantly. We may witness to Christ living within us and to God's capacity to help us become loving and patient and mature; or we may witness to our own resistance to God's truth and to our selfishness and immaturity. A proper Christian witness is when we live out, in our relationships with others, God's love to each of us. Effective witness does not require explaining the plan of salvation in every conversation or to admonish another person for every fault we might imagine we see within him. For myself, I am not comfortable giving any confrontation or spiritual admonition or evangelistic statement without a clear sense of God's direction.

4. If you can trust me, I will be dependable, even though I may not be predictable. The things I do in order to serve you may surprise you; the consistency of my servanthood will please you.

Clara and Henry were married 57 years and Clara's eyes sparkled as she talked about it. "Trust? Oh, yes, that's an important part of a good marriage. But it's funny, trust is." She paused and stared intently at the large-print Bible lying on her lap. "You see, it took me 30 or 40 years to learn how much I could trust Henry.

"I'll tell you what I mean." Her eyes were misty for the man she longed to see, but danced in tribute to the strength of their love.

"For years and years we scrimped hard to make it. I kept track of every penny, or tried to, because it seemed like there was always a little I couldn't account for. I never had any reason to distrust Henry, not in any way. Never. In any way. But it seemed like over the years always some money trickled off into nowhere. Every week. I tried not to worry about it, but it sure did puzzle me.

"Well, when our youngest got married—we had five, you know—when she got married and it was all over, Henry came in and he had two expensive train tickets and he said, 'You and me are going on a honeymoon, too.' There were all those pennies!

"Yes, he could be trusted, yes indeed. He was always there in the way that was right for me even though lots of times it wasn't in the way I expected. He was always that way."

And you knew she wouldn't have changed a moment of it. Rock-solid trust with creativity—just what you'd want for every marriage.

5. *If you can trust me, our conversations are confidential—just for us. If I talk with others about you it is not to entertain them, it is to affirm you.*

Nothing could be added to that to enhance the importance of it. Let us merely add that confidentiality means that we do not gossip in giving prayer requests, that we do not say more to members of the other person's family than they would have us say to anyone else, and that we don't talk about others—even if we haven't identified them by name or by some other way.

6. *If you can trust me, our relationship will strengthen you—lead you to confident independence. We may be dependent on one another from time to time because of our needs and in the mutual joy that comes in serving one another, but I will not seek to control you. My strength is used to support you.*

Margaret wanted to be the perfect mother. She did everything she could do for her children except one thing—teach them how to do things for themselves. When the two children left home there were six persons whose lives were suddenly out of control: two children who could scarcely butter their own bread, Margaret who lost her purpose in life, and three frustrated spouses.

We should nudge others toward greater responsibility, but not too fast. Gene was a recovering alcoholic. Bright, witty, handsome and likeable, he seemed a natural to help others. The alcoholism treatment agency in his state hired him and he was successful. He was promoted and they expected more of him. He produced. They wanted more. The pressure began to be more than he could handle so . . . drinking again, marital conflict, more drinking, divorce, drinking, fighting, jail.

He had been abused by the very system that had

helped him. They sinned against him by pushing him into responsibility faster than he could handle it. They used him as an object and wore him out.

As your servant friend I will help you grow up. I will nudge, not shove, and I will keep watching to see if what I do is for your benefit.

These are characteristics of a person who can be trusted, but a description is not enough. How do we develop the integrity and unselfishness that characterize trustworthiness?

It's a lifelong process and most of the things mentioned in this book contribute to it. But three things are essential.

First is to love God. Jesus said, "Love the Lord your God with all your soul and with all your mind" (see Matt. 22:37-39). Loving God is the one area of life in which we should try for perfection because we can only love others and ourselves in proportion to our love for God. We can only rise above the threats, losses, frustrations and rejections of life to the extent that we trust God, and we can only trust God to the extent that we understand His love for us; so it is understandable that Jesus described that commandment as the first and greatest. As we love and trust God we can become more other-centered and develop a life view from which we reflexively look out for the best interests of others.

The second foundational condition is to *seek to understand the other person.* We understand others as we listen. We show our respect and concern for others as we give up the Verbal Villains or other barriers to servant friendship and concentrate on accurate listening, as we talk less about our own concerns and encourage other persons to tell us about themselves.

The third foundational condition is to *be vulnerable.* We cannot force others to trust us—we can only give it. Trust comes through sharing and investing ourselves into others, even though we may be hurt from it.

Self-disclosure is one of the ways in which we invite trust. As we gradually remove protective shells from ourselves by telling others who we are, we put some of our security in their hands. This builds trust by giving trust.

Trust is necessary if we are to really know and serve one another. Trust is fragile and when we break trust, even one, it may take 10 or more trusting acts to regain credibility. This is where a willingness to apologize and to forgive comes in. If it is hard to trust, it probably is harder to apologize or forgive; but God dependably and generously helps us so that these acts build trust.

When our relationship comes to a point of mutual trust, we will celebrate—with fireworks, balloons, singing and dancing in the streets—for now we can help one another spontaneously, fully, vigorously in our movement toward personal effectiveness. One of the first things we'll do when the celebration settles down is to let ourselves be known more completely to one another through self-disclosure.

Discussion Questions

1. What underlying feelings do you sense in Haley's beginning remarks about the church's helping the refugee family?
2. Describe Rose's character as portrayed in this chapter. Is she an effective servant friend to her husband?
3. Discuss the paragraphs on physical intimacy. What insights can you add for Christians on this topic?
4. Explore these verses in regard to having respect for other persons: Proverbs 25:8-10; Luke 14:10,11; Romans 12:16; Ephesians 4:25; Philippians 2:3,4; James 2:9; 1 Peter 2:17.
5. Check these verses in regard to confidentiality: Proverbs 11:13; 20:19; James 1:26; 4:11,12.

Chapter Nine

Letting You Know Me: Self-Disclosure

by Daniel J. Siemasko

Hello, human, across the street, mowing your lawn. How are you, besides bright blue, plaid, and busy?

That orange mower sure makes a lot of noise for an electric. You can't hear my typewriter saying "hello," can you? Hello! *HELLO!!!* You have no idea I'm looking from my window trying to connect. Yet we are connected, my electric typewriter linked somehow with your electric mower.

We look alike: two arms, two legs, body, and head. We live near each other. We're neighbors. But I don't know anything more than that about you. I don't know your name. I don't know how you feel. You know what else we have in common? We're both avoiders.

Why do I reach out to you, a stranger, now? You've been there for years.

The peppy humming of your machine makes me think you're really into grass cutting. Are you? Are you really lost in your mowing pattern? Is landscaping something you hope to get into? I ask because I guess I want you to ask me what I'm doing. I want to tell someone who I am. I want to

be known! Not famous, just understood and accepted.
Next best, I would prefer to be left alone, as it is now. I
don't want to take a chance at being laughed at.

I just took another look at your lawn and I had this wild
thought. What if you were carving a big "hello" in your
yard? I'd rush to meet you! Or maybe not. Maybe I'd think
you were nuts!

Why is part of me hoping you'll stay away and part of
me wishing we'd be closer?

What Is Self-Disclosure? Self-disclosure is telling
another person about yourself. It's showing yourself:

—what you are and are not
—what you have and need
—what you want and hope for
—what you've learned and dreamed
—what you like and don't like
—what you think and feel
—what you believe and doubt
—what your talents and shortcomings are
—what you fantasize and really do
— what you're challenged by and fearful of
—what successes and failures you've had
—what commitments and plans you've made.

In short, you're revealing what God has made important
to you.

Self-disclosure can be very enjoyable because it lets
me be the center of attention. If we take turns talking about
ourselves, we both enjoy. But, who's going to go first?

"Go ahead, *you* disclose."

"No, *you*."

"Why don't we think this over carefully: should we or
shouldn't we?"

Let's Not

Why should we open up at all? After all, it's so safe this
way, you in your Bermuda shorts pushing your machine

around your turf, and me sitting up here writing about friendship.

I would think of all kinds of reasons to stay apart, minding our own business. For one, although I want to be known, I'm afraid to show my real face. Right now only I know who I really am. If I share that with you, and you don't like it, what might happen? I might shock you. Sidney Jourard in *The Transparent Self* suggests that "Many of us dread to be known by others as intimately as we know ourselves because we would be divorced, imprisoned or shot."[1]

I fear you would think me weak. Perhaps I should "grin and bear it, keep a stiff upper lip, and suffer in silence." That's what I've been told many times, and I've done it; but, oh how it hurts! There must be a better way—but maybe you wouldn't agree.

Another reason to not disclose is that you might not care about me. With so many real troubles in the world, why would you be interested in my petty matters? And, to be honest, who cares what *you* think? I would enjoy talking about me, but I'd rather not listen to you. So, why should we trouble each other?

And if I did let you in on my soft spots, you'd probably end up jumping on them. I may want to share, but I don't trust you. But don't take it personally; I wouldn't tell anyone everything. Opening is scary, Jourard states, because when you let yourself be known "you expose yourself not only to a lover's balm, but also to a hater's bombs!"[2] Your "friend" knows where to plant them for maximum effect.

What if I started to expose my essence and you misunderstood? Or worse yet, understood so well what's wrong with me. You might hold me accountable—confront me with the need to change, expect me to use my abilities, look for continuing maturity. That would be good for me, but it might not be comfortable.

Jesuit Father John Powell points out that it's tough to deal with emotional honesty: "We would rather defend our dishonesty on the grounds that it might hurt others; and, having rationalized our phoniness into nobility, settle for superficial relationships."[3]

I have to admit, though, that all the reasons I have to stay closed don't tip the scale against my one feeling on the other side, my idea that what I have, what I am, is supposed to be shared.

Let's

What do we have to gain? A deeper, more meaningful friendship. Although we have the potential to hurt our relationship, we can help it. Sure it will be risky. But if we have more to gain than all we know we can lose, it's worth the gamble.

We'll get to know each other more completely. The understanding we'll share will be based more on our authentic selves and less on our masked and acted roles. That lays the foundation for us to begin to trust enough to give and receive the acceptance and help we both need.

Powell says, "There is in each of us a deep and driving desire to be understood."[4] Clark Moustakas writes, "At bottom, each person wants to be rescued and helped out of his terror and deceit."[5] And it is that need for relationship with God and other persons that is repeated over and over in the Bible.

Self-disclosure helps me develop as a person; it is a vote of confidence on behalf of myself because when I let you know who I am, I show you that I believe that I am worthwhile. And it helps you, too; for when you show me that you can be trusted with my self-disclosure—when you are interested in what interests me and when you treat me with respect and caring when I talk about my faults and failures—I feel accepted and can more fully accept you. That makes the bond between us much stronger.

I'll let you know me and where I'm at. You'll tell me about yourself. I'll let you see life from my angle, and you'll show me your view. I'll tell you how I feel about you and see how you feel about me. We'll share our self-information on life and our original suggestions for living. I'll begin by saying, "I've never told anyone this before," and you'll reply, "I never knew anyone felt these same things." Unexploited vulnerability will encourage more openness between ourselves and model healthy relationships for others. They'll see people trusting other people. Imagine where that could lead!

My Experiment with Self-Disclosure

I didn't know how closed I was until I experienced openness and the subsequent and continuing, long and steady, God-controlled process of coming to trust others.

I was outside of God for 15 years—from the time my mother stopped making me go to church until I first experienced people open with people.

As a radio recording engineer I found myself inducted into the church's service. In another way I was a volunteer. Although I was a conscientious objector to the Jesus promotion, it turned out that no one on the engineering staff but I cared to sit through the prerecording sessions of the Sunday night sermons. For the others it was like being in church more than once a week. For me, no problem. As a non-churchgoer I was the most talented in tuning the stuff out. I was probably exposed to more preaching than any person on earth and still I was untouched. I heard all that faith, hope, and irrelevancy when I was a kid and the issue was dead. I didn't need a fairy tale to keep me in line. Once I got my audio levels set on the control board and the preacher was rolling, I'd turn down my monitor to an undistracting background murmur, prop up my feet, and open some meaty philosophical reading. In a way, the "Jesus shows" were my favorite times of the week.

Angel food all sounded the same. Only one show was different enough to be distracting. "Experiments in Faith"[6] was low in clichés and pretense and high in honesty and humanness. Guests on the talk show spoke of fear, doubt, selfishness, and failing as their problems. I always thought the churched were supposed to pretend, for the sake of their own belief and for the irritation of non-believers, that things like reality didn't exist.

As distracting as "Experiments" was, however, it wasn't very interesting to listen to until I began to eavesdrop. While I racked up my tapes in the control booth I was able to throw a switch to those in the studio as they prepared and listen in without their knowing. Unlike the customary, "I'll read this poem, we'll play this hymn, you read John 3:16, then I'll do my 'God's love' homily for the remaining 26 minutes," "Experiments in Faith" had an unusual preparation. They'd pray, unusual prayers. For instance, I'd see two guys go into the studio and hear two talk to a third: "If I could just say what I mean" or "Lord, it's been a crazy day; slow me down." They'd even kid around and laugh in prayer, talking with God with the same kind of freedom you'd have in asking your best friend for a drink of water.

This intrigued me enough to listen in to the show once in a while, which led to a more friendly relationship in the studio, which later led to their inviting me to one of their weekend small group gatherings. I accepted. Why? Maybe because I wanted a chance to blow the most respectable of the religious out of the water with my accumulation of logic. It wasn't because I trusted them. And it surely wasn't because I needed anything. I made that clear from the beginning: "I'm here, but I don't need it."

The first night at the conference everyone was paired up. I was one-on-one with a veteran "Experimenter." The program's ice-breaker was "Tell the other person who you are and why you're here." I went first: "I'm Dan Siemasko

and I don't need anything." I knew this Christian was
going to lay the answer on me when he got his turn, so I
used as much time as I could displaying my wisdom. In the
remaining space he got to make three points, none of
which I expected.

One, he said he wasn't very happy about being at the
weekend "retreat." He came because he had nowhere
else to talk. Two, something about his relationship with his
18-year-old daughter was troubling him. And three,
seems he had some steam to release about his having
been arrested and held behind bars the weekend before.

I didn't know what to say. Here I am barricaded behind my thick wall of defense, my gun sticking out of the
one and only tiny opening, and in my sights I see this guy
looking at me as if I could help.

Wow, did my posture change fast! I had to admit that I
didn't have his answer, nor did I have one of my own. It
was retreat time for both of us.

From then on, as I recorded "Experiments in Faith"
every week, I used my tiny opening to listen. I heard a lot
of dependent people who from all outward appearances
were most independent. It wasn't long before I was comfortable enough to ask them, "If you're so practical, why
do you need the Jesus crutch? Why do you keep relying
on the myth?" My salvation began there where it had to
start, in my unbelief, with my cynicism, at my point of
need. The myth met me where I was.

One sort of milestone that occurred about four years
later epitomizes the kind of effect open people had on me.
The paragraph will seem like a simple composition without
the actual long pauses and deep tremors between the
phrases. This was the first time I trusted me to tell me
something. Through Christ, I discovered my own opinion
and saw the position I got myself into. From a note I
scratched one day in the recording studio, I transcribe for
you the feelings I had behind my wall:

There's first this enormous feeling of not being wanted. Not needed, not useful, not appreciated, not respected, without worth, in the way. The professionalism I've grown so far for is no longer acknowledged. There's no recognition. There's no involvement—no sense of participating. There's no room to grow. There's nothing. No way to get better at what I'm doing. I'm bored. And resentful of the management which is negligent enough or conspiring enough to allow this to happen.

The time came when each week I'd pray openly with those of "Experiments in Faith" before the recording. An eavesdrop grew into my leading them in prayer. The spirit of Christ made it through a double-glass, double-door, acoustically-sealed studio, and through the tiny hole in the thick wall where a weapon used to wait.

God's Openness

Anyone who knows Jesus knows just how interested the Father is in meeting our individual needs. He wants to hear what's important to us and one of the ways He gets us to disclose our true concerns is by telling us of Himself.

The Bible is God's self-disclosure. In it He lets us know who He is, what He feels, what He hopes for, and what commitments He's made. As untheological as this may sound, I sense His doubts, needs, and fears. I look at the note I wrote and can imagine Him writing it. "Hey, I love you so much I gave my only Son for you—that's who I am."

And Jesus: "How much I've longed to gather you all together, as a hen gathers her chicks under her wings, but you're not willing." And He weeps, further disclosing the God He is.

Paul shares his personal experiences, Peter his visions,

and David his all in Psalms. By telling us of themselves, they're encouraging our disclosure: "Tell each other your faults so that you may be healed."

The Specifics of Appropriate Self-Disclosure

Turn these title words around and we make the important point: Self-disclosure is a matter of being appropriately specific. The following thoughts summarize the use and misuse of self-disclosure:

Here and Now. Generally, the closer we are personally and the closer we are in time to the event being disclosed, the greater is our degree of interaction. We could have a mild exchange about someone else's family long ago or we could talk about a happening in our family this morning. Or we could share how we feel right now. The closer we get to first person present, the more intense is our communication—of course, the greater the risk and reluctance too.

Under most conditions it's better to use a lower intensity self-disclosure first and allow the intensity to rise naturally. Don't be bashful; but on the other hand, don't jump in too fast.

Relevant. What you talk about should be of interest to both of you, and not you alone. You can still share yourself, but include your reactions and opinions about things he or she is interested in. Watch the other person's attention as a rough measure of how relevant you're being. If the other person doesn't look interested, she or he probably is not. Be careful; time goes quickly when we are talking about ourselves. Learn to leave at least 60 percent of the time for the other person.

Spontaneous. Self-disclosure should come from a spirit of wanting to know and be known. If it's used mechanically or "on schedule" or as a technique, it won't have much benefit and may be detrimental to the relationship.

Controlled. It's a misuse of self-disclosure to invade others' privacy by being inappropriately intimate. This is to manipulate the other persons into telling you intimate things about themselves. You tell your secrets, and then, in effect, say to them, "I've spilled my guts, now it's your turn." You're making an unfair demand on them.

There are many things in the life of each of us that do not need to be shared: the sins of the past, once confessed to and forgiven by God, should rarely be discussed; many things are too trivial to be useful to others; we should avoid wallowing in our present confusions or discouragements. An excess of self-disclosure can be as destructive as too little, leading to over-familiarity, reduced personal identity, and boring self-directedness. Before disclosing ask yourself, "Is it useful to me or to them to talk about this?"

Helpful. Keep your self-disclosure directed at helping the other person. The other person's needs are changing all the time. Yours will be too. Keep checking yourself on the purpose of your self-disclosure. Don't disclose until you know what the other person's needs are.

Don't assume that what has happened to you is very much like what happened to the other guy. Stories may start out the same for the first couple of paragraphs but may end up vastly different. Allow for that. Don't jump to conclusions. Also, just to show that you know that your life experience is not exactly the same as that of the other person, you might preface your own story with something like this: "I know that what happened to me is not exactly the same as what happened to you, but there seems to be some similarity, enough that maybe you would be interested in hearing what happened to me."

Thanks for Being There

Whether to disclose our authentic being or to conceal it—the choice is sometimes tough. Theory indicates that we should open up, but practice often warns us against it.

The key seems to be knowing when to be appropriately open. Just rely on your genuineness, the reality that surfaces when you rely on the Holy Spirit.

I still haven't talked to my grass-cutting neighbor. Much bitterness remains unreported after my 12 painful years in broadcasting (I left a year ago). My 14-year-old daughter is afraid to be frank with me. I still can't open up without feeling like I'm trying to manipulate the other person (you, in this case). I look at the Jesus-like listeners who serve me and wonder why I can't be like them. Why am I always so concerned about me? I read the ideals I've enumerated here and tremble as I ask myself, who are you trying to fool?

As I tell you of my shakiness, I feel my rock-bottom base; I sense the presence of Christ. Yes, I have a lot of fear and doubt about myself, yet greater is my confidence. I'm going to make it! But I wasn't sure until you were there to listen. Thank you.

Discussion Questions

1. Can you identify with the writer's need to reach out to the stranger—his neighbor mowing the lawn—and yet his reluctance? How would you tackle the task of getting that friendship started?
2. What are the main reasons for our feeling hesitant toward self-disclosure?
3. What is to be gained by tactful self-disclosure? Give an experience of your own to illustrate.
4. Discuss the five "specifics" of self-disclosure.

Notes
1. Sidney M. Jourard, *The Transparent Self* (New York: D. Van Nostrand Co., 1971), p. 59.
2. Ibid, p. 5.
3. John Powell, S.J., *Why Am I Afraid to Tell You Who I Am?* (Niles, IL: Argus Communications, 1969), p. 88.
4. Ibid, p. 95.
5. Clark I. Moustakas, *Individuality and Encounter* (Cambridge, Mass: Howard A. Doyle Publishing Co., 1973), p. 55.
6. Presented by the Pittsburgh Experiment.

Chapter Ten

Telling It the Way It Is, Lovingly: Confrontation

"Bang! Bang!" From an apartment balcony a nine-year-old boy fired a toy rifle at his mother who was getting into her car at the curb below. "Bang! Bang!" He lowered the weapon and, with narrowed eyes, studied his quarry.

She paused. "Go inside." Her voice penetrated like a cold steel blade. "Lock the door. Stay inside so you don't get hurt." She meant it, and she waited.

He raised and sighted his gun, and pumped a few more bullets into her. Then, slowly and reluctantly, yet with a twitch of cocky triumph, he went inside to stay alone.

The scene was brief, intense, private, painful to watch. I was in the back seat of the car as we drove away in awkward silence. "What does this imitation murder mean?" I thought to myself.

Is it an honest plea for attention? Does the mock assault *really* mean "I love you, Mom—don't leave me"?

Is it merely a harmless outlet for a child's enthusiasm? The needed discharge of energy from a boy with gusto?

Is it hatred? Is it saying, "I'll get you for this! This is just a sample of the pain I'm going to give you in one way or another when I'm big enough!"?

His mother drove quickly through the misty, darkening city. In the rearview mirror I could see tense furrows above soft, intelligent eyes that, while they scanned for potholes along the rough, narrow street, seemed at the same time to be looking inward.

"How would she explain this?" I thought. Perhaps she would say, "This is just part of what I've always tried to help him with—being expressive. I'm giving him the freedom to be himself. He has imagination! He has creativity! I'm glad for that. I'm not going to press him into a tight little coffin of conformity, killing his spirit and forcing him to endure a living death!"

That must be it—she doesn't want to get in the way of her son's growing up—she wants him to live fully, with vigor and freedom. "If that's her goal," I thought, "how Christian." It was a goal I could endorse.

But her means of helping her son live—how futile! For life comes not from freedom to express one's self, but from Christ being expressed through us.

And her willingness to die, even symbolically, that her son might live—how unnecessary! For Christ died that each of us might live, that we might have life and have it abundantly, HALLELUJAH!

Earlier that evening she hadn't wanted to hear about Christ's love. She had thrown too much time and money at the feet of false prophets of pop-psychology to listen to Jesus. To listen to Jesus would be to admit having been wrong. "Being wrong is weakness," she had said. "I'm me. I'm right. I'm right because I'm me."

My thoughts were interrupted as she began to speak, loud against the thunder and rain. "It was healthy for him to vent his frustration. He let go of his anger on the balcony. He left it outside." Our eyes met in the mirror. "He's okay back at the apartment. He's having a good time. I've taught him to express himself. That's all that happened. That's what I wanted. That's good."

A burst of rain bullets jolted the car. She murmured, to no one in particular, "And yet . . ."

It was a time of confrontations. There are two important definitions of the word "confrontation." One meaning is "an incident of hostility or opposition between people." The incident between the boy and his mother was that kind of confrontation—one that divides.

Confrontation also means "to bring together face to face for examination or comparison." Again, there may be opposition—between behaviors, attitudes, or beliefs rather than between persons—but not necessarily hostility. This kind of confrontation helps persons become aware of oppositions that hurt them—it points out factors that divide, as a way of strengthening the person. We examine that kind of confrontation in this chapter.

Earlier in the evening this woman had described her search for happiness, a feverish life-style in opposition to God's truth and the cool water offered in salvation. I had confronted her by summarizing what she had said so the great gap between her efforts and the results was clear. It was a mild confrontation and she ignored it.

The purpose of confrontation is constructive change in the life of the confronted person. That can begin only after the person accepts that oppositions exist within his or her life and that they should be changed. Our task is to present the truth; only the other person can accept and apply the truth. The process often takes time. When she murmured "And yet . . ." perhaps she was beginning to recognize the oppositions within her and was about to confront herself with the need to change. Perhaps, and yet . . .

Confrontation is a powerful force for better or worse. It can lead to constructive change and growth or to greater defensiveness by the confronted person. It can cement the relationship or shatter it, as Paul found out: "Have I now become your enemy by telling you the truth?" (Gal. 4:16)

Confrontation is an act of love. The confronter is not

willing for the other person to live with discrepancies that end only in destruction. The confronter will not let the other person go on trying to live out a life-style that defies social, physical, or spiritual realities. The confronter will not sit idly by, fire extinguisher in hand, while his neighbor burns his own house down.

Confrontation seeks to help the other person have more accurate self-understanding. The confronter does as much as is possible through listening and observing, praying, and studying to understand before trying to teach understanding.

Confrontation is unselfish. It is a sharing of the worthwhile realities of life that we have learned. Our personal survival has depended upon others who have, by confronting us, protected us from our own foolishness and ignorance. We give to others as we pass truth along.

Confrontation puts limits on the relationship. It states that you do not fully accept something about the other person's behavior, beliefs, or attitudes. To some extent you are rejecting part of the other person. This can be painful to them and scary for you to do because you wonder if you may be rejected in return.

Confrontation must be done with caution and flexibility. It often requires impact to wake the person up, to arouse slumbering energy. It may take some brute force to move coasting habits into new directions. But at the same time it needs finesse, recognizing that human beings are fragile and can be painfully broken. The confronter makes several decisions about confrontation style: to be direct or indirect, to confront now or later, to be tough or gentle. The discerning confronter distinguishes between the tough hide of defense and tender ego nerves; the flexible confronter can jab the one and soothe the other.

Confrontation is an act of courage. Confrontations often strain the relationship temporarily. The confronter may be ignored, rebuffed, ridiculed, or attacked—any or all. The confronter recognizes and accepts the risk and attempts to keep it to a minimum.

Confrontation is an investment in the future. For the time being it is easier to not confront because people often deny or resist the message that is being given them. There may not be any benefit for a long time.

Confrontation is an uncomfortable act for many persons. Knowing that the confronted person might be a little tense often creates tension in the confronter. Confrontations that are avoided or postponed are usually more difficult to do later.

Confrontation must be an act of integrity. Because entering into another person's life is risky, doing it can be motivated only out of pathology or out of love. The confronted person will quickly know from which motive it comes. Confrontation must resist dirtying the relationship with condescension or resentment. It must discern between punishment and discipline, right and wrong, justice and mercy.

Confrontation is an act of vibrant optimism. The confronter becomes deeply involved in the life of the other person as a way of challenging that person to become deeply involved in his or her own life. It is the confronter's way of saying, "Life is good—so good that I'm not willing for you to half live your life!"

Confrontation is an opportunity for the confronter to grow by working through a difficult relational task; to discover that obedience to the Lord always is better.

Confrontation must be an act in cooperation with God so that our selfishness is supplanted by servanthood, vengeance by forgiveness, and competitiveness by teamwork—enabling confrontation to be for the benefit of the other person.

Confrontation is an act of Christian obedience. The Bible presents it as part of responsibility within the body of believers. We are to warn (see 1 Thess. 5:14), rebuke and teach (see 2 Tim. 4:2), and encourage (see Heb. 3:13) for the purpose of restoring the other (see Gal. 6:1). "Speaking the truth in love" (Eph. 4:15; see also v. 25) is a corporate responsibility through seeing that truth is taught and through discipline with the body of believers.

Confrontation is often difficult. It may be because a person lacks knowledge and skills. These are important, so the fundamentals are covered in this chapter. But attitude is far more important and the attitude must be one of tough love.

Tough love refuses to let another person stay on a self-destructive course. Often we don't have tough love, and that's why we don't confront people. Our love is not tough enough to knock somebody down and stay there to pick him back up, brush the dust off him, and then walk down the road with him.

Our love is weak. We look for peace at any cost. We say to ourselves, "I can't confront him because he won't be my friend anymore." Or we think, "She'll leave me if I confront her about this issue."

Love is seeking the other person's highest good. It means being concerned about the best interests of the other person, being "your brother's keeper." That's a responsibility each of us has.

If you don't confront a friend, you simply don't love that friend as much as you might. Confrontation is an essential part of love. Love without confrontation is weak, incomplete, insufficient to meet the needs of the other person. So the motivation for confrontation is love—nothing more, nothing less. Confrontation is love because through your confrontation the other person might change, might grow, might be healed, might stop a self-destructive pattern, stop hurting others, or abandon a sin in his or her life.

A question for us to ask ourselves is: Do I love people enough to take the risk of confrontation with the goal that it will bring something more beautiful into their lives? If you must say no to that, go back to chapter 2. If you can say yes, keep reading as we look at the "how to's" of confrontation in three parts: message, preparation, and method.

Message

We defined confrontation as the process of helping another person understand how oppositions—let's call them "discrepancies"—in his or her life can be hurtful. These discrepancies may be within one person's own system: words or behavior in the past versus words or behavior at the present; goals or beliefs versus behavior; or a goal or belief that is in conflict with another goal or belief.

Or the discrepancies may be between a part of the person's system and some part of another system. There are many possible combinations:

his/her perceptions or goals or
behavior or beliefs or attitudes

versus

God's laws or social laws or standards or preferences of other persons or rights of other persons
or laws of nature

For example, Larry says that he wants to make good grades but he doesn't study. This is a discrepancy between his stated goal, good grades, and his behavior—not studying.

Lois says that she doesn't need friends, that she can get along without other people in her life. She may believe this but it defies what Scripture teaches us about the importance of other people in a meaningful life.

Max says the speed limit is 55 miles per hour so he drives 55 even though the road is icy. There is a predictable conflict between this behavior and the laws of nature. If Max has a goal of staying alive then this behavior, given the laws of nature, is not consistent with that goal.

The most common reason people have such discrepancies is because they are influenced by more than one motivator. Larry does want good grades but he also wants the friendship of his peers, so he hangs around with them instead of studying. Lois, not understanding that people will like her, allows excessive fear to overrule her desire to be with others. Max wants prestige from his job—he wants to be his company's national sales leader. He drives fast so he can make more calls. The goal is fine, but not worth the risk to his life.

The message of a confrontation is to point out such discrepancies, to bring them together face to face for examination. You can build up another person through effective confrontation, but it requires careful preparation.

Preparation

The first thing we need to do is pray. Then the second thing we need to do is pray. And the third thing we need to do is pray. Then we need to pray some more. Why? Because we need to be sure our confrontation is for the benefit of the other person. Pray for wisdom, self-control, discernment, a sense of timing, and for the right perspective.

Prayer is the most important part of preparation, but preparation begins with listening to the other person, and that begins at the introduction and never stops. The acceptance we show—through listening, through affirmation, through the trust that develops, through sharing in self-disclosure—is the foundational process that should occur before confrontation. As we do those things we get acquainted with the person and begin to see the discrepancies in his or her life.

Because confrontation carries risk, we need to earn the right to impose that risk into the confronted person's life. One way we get the right is from friendship. Part of a full friendship is a responsibility to prevent each other from self-inflicted hurt. In a full friendship we give each other permission to "tell it like it is" when that is beneficial.

Another way of getting the right is if the other person is actively seeking our advice or insight into his own situation. And a third is when we are in a position of authority and responsibility for the other such as a parent, teacher, employer, or organizational officer.

The success or failure of confrontation usually depends on the quality of relationship between the two persons before the confrontation. The more accurate our listening, the more accurate our confrontation will probably be.

The more clearly we have shown love in other situations, the easier it will be for the confronted person to forgive us for the blunders that we will probably make as we show love in the form of confrontation. The more we have trusted that person the more trust he will have in what we say and the more likely he is to take it seriously.

We should check out the message of our confrontation against Scripture. There may be times when we should check it out with another person. We need to check our own motivation for confronting. Here are some questions that, if we ask ourselves before confronting, will help us keep mistakes to a minimum:

Is confrontation the right technique? Have I listened, spent time with him, been friendly? Do I have the right to confront? Have I proved I can be trusted?

Is the other person ready? Can he benefit from the message? How will it affect others, such as the confronted person's family?

Is my confrontation as accurate as possible? Am I jumping to conclusions? Have I done all I can to understand the circumstances and the person?

Is my own act together? Is this for me or for the other person? Have I been fair, reliable, and caring? Am I practicing what I preach? Do I owe him an apology for my offenses to him? Do I have a plan?

Method

The more you lean on someone the more likely he is to push back. Confrontation leans on the other person. The confrontation can be so weak as to be unnoticed or so harsh as to be destructive to the person and to provoke him to anger. The confrontation needs to be intense enough to get attention and yet not so intense as to antagonize, to unnecessarily raise defenses or to destroy relationships.

In between those extremes lies quite a range of intensity from a gentle and low-risk style to a tough style with higher risk. Often we choose to start with a gentle style and see if that works. If it does, fine; but if it doesn't we can increase the intensity until we get the job done. If we start with tough intensity we may lose the whole opportunity.

A gentle style gives the receiver a chance to avoid facing the facts of the discrepancy; a tough style closes the exits. A gentle style hints while a tough style boldly states the message in black and white. A gentle style is quite supportive, but the tough style "leans" on the receiver. To illustrate, let's look at an example:

Joyce and Brenda were having coffee in the teachers' lounge of Fillmore Elementary. Every time Joyce looked at Brenda she was reminded of what Charley had said, "Being around Brenda gives me a bellyful of pine cones."

She'd laughed the first time she'd heard it, for she knew the feeling. But she also knew Brenda and she knew about the abrupt, painful divorce that lay behind her complaining and her fears. Still, it was hard now for Joyce to keep her mind on what Brenda was saying—she'd heard it all before, over and over again.

"It's a terrible time to try to sell a house, but I can't afford to keep it. I can't do the yard work and . . ."

It was the end of a long day. Joyce wanted to kick herself for getting trapped with Brenda, yet felt a tinge of guilt about that feeling. After all, she thought, they were in the same fellowship group at church and she knew that this friendship was both a responsibility to Brenda and an opportunity for Joyce's own personal growth.

The friendship had been frustrating. At first Joyce had listened and listened, but over the months it hadn't seemed to have had much helpful effect. Brenda continued to complain about the same things, to vent her anger about her ex-husband, to talk about the humiliation she had felt, to describe her fears of the future, and to coax for reassurance and sympathy. One by one the others at school and at church began avoiding Brenda. Joyce's commitment as a Christian would not let her do that, but she had not found anything constructive to do.

Then she began to realize that Brenda's complaining was not just a symptom of her problem but was beginning to be a problem in itself, and knew that it needed to change. She thought of this as a counseling job and didn't feel prepared to handle it, but she could not justify allowing Brenda to go on without doing what she could to help her with it.

Today Joyce was feeling a sense of desperation and panic. She thought of the pile of papers on her desk that hadn't been graded last week because she was listening to Brenda. She felt angry. Impatience suddenly swept through her.

She blurted, " Brenda, stop just a minute! Stop! Please listen to me for just a minute! I don't want to be rude, but I just don't have time to listen; I've got lots to do. I'd like to stay but I don't have time."

"Just a minute more. There's one more thing I need to tell you."

"No, I don't have time."

"You have to listen to this."

"No, I don't have to. I'm sick and tired of you telling me I've got to sit around and listen to all your griping. I know it was terrible for you to have Jack leave. That's a more rugged thing to have happen to you than anything I've ever had happen to me. I've listened to you tell how awful it was and I've listened again and again and again. I've tried to be helpful to you by my listening; but good grief!

"Everybody's got a limit and I think you've pushed me way past mine. You've got to consider other people. It isn't doing you any good to let you complain and complain until you drive everyone away from you. You need to start giving to others instead of just taking, taking, taking.

"Brenda, you're not going to get over this thing until you decide that you don't have a right to insist that other people listen to you!"

"See? Nobody cares! That's what I was just saying!" Brenda jumped to her feet, trembling, tears spilling out of her eyes. "I wasn't insisting! I thought you were my friend. I thought you were different than everybody else. If you don't want me around, that's easy to take care of!" She ran from the room.

Joyce walked slowly back to her own room, gathered up her papers, and went home. She was bewildered, felt defeated, and was sure she had handled it in the worst possible way.

Not so. This was a "tough" confrontation and was effective. It is not a typical textbook example because it has flaws in it; we might second-guess some aspects of Joyce's style. But she had done several things right: she was honest, specific and clear, showed that she was aware of Brenda's problems, and the information she gave was accurate and potentially useful. To see why it was effective, in spite of the flaws, we must look at what had preceded this conversation.

Joyce had spent a great deal of time listening to Brenda. This showed respect, proved her caring, and helped her have a well-informed, objective perspective on Brenda. She had earned the right to confront.

Along the way she realized that Brenda needed to be told that her repetitive complaining and demands were destructive to herself and to her friendships. This was the message. The listening was part of Joyce's preparation, but also she prayed about confronting Brenda, thought about it, and decided that Brenda's behavior was inconsistent with the ideal pattern of Christian relationships. Over a period of several weeks Joyce had used several approaches to confronting Brenda.

A weak confrontation. She began by dropping hints. "I think I've heard that before."

"Oh, yes. I'm sorry. I shouldn't bore you with all that. It's just that . . ." Brenda went on to say it again.

"Well, maybe I shouldn't say anything, since you are one of my favorite people, but this does kinda seem repetitious."

"You haven't heard this. Tomorrow I must . . ."

Joyce wanted to scream. But she interrupted to say, "I didn't mean to be critical."

A hint is fine, if it works. This time it didn't. Brenda, like most people in distress, was so wrapped up in her own problem she did not catch the hint.

Weak confrontations are apologetic and vague. They are given in a lighthearted "I'm your pal" nonverbal style that is inconsistent with the seriousness of the message. They may mingle in so much good news with the bad news that the confronted person doesn't even notice the important message. This has no constructive effect and may even result in loss of respect for the confronter, or even reinforce the discrepancy by giving the impression that the discrepancy isn't important.

Weak confrontations are a sign of a fearful or uncaring confronter. They may come from lack of confidence in the message itself, in one's ability to justify it, or an effort to deny the discrepancy exists.

A harsh confrontation. Joyce exploded in rage one day. "It's no wonder you feel so miserable, the way you are pouting and whining and feeling sorry for yourself all the time. I don't know how you can have any self-respect when you act that way. It's no wonder that other people don't like to be around you."

Brenda felt scolded and rejected, and burst into tears. Joyce immediately put her arm around her.

"I'm sorry. I've been cross all day. I didn't know what I was saying. I've been yelling at my class like this too. It's awful of me. Forget I said it; it's not true."

But it was true. Truth was there, but not love. The message was accurate but presented in such a harsh way that Brenda heard only the absence of love, not the presence of truth.

A harsh confrontation condemns not behavior or beliefs but the actual person. It rejects and punishes instead of trying to understand and reeducate. This style may include inflammatory words, threats, and other rage behavior, or may be cold, indifferent and cynical.

Harsh confrontations usually build walls between persons, may cause the confronted person to go on the attack, avoid the confronter or pretend to accept the message but to ignore it when the confronter is gone.

Harsh confrontations generally are given by confronters who have personal deficits such as unresolved hostility or frustration, have little empathy or respect for others, and are calloused about the effects they have on others. They may give the confronter a temporary sense of power or release of tension, but these benefits don't last long because they are at the expense of the other person. In the long run, harsh confrontations are destructive to the giver as well as to the receiver.

A gentle confrontation. Joyce used self-disclosure appropriately, hoping Brenda would learn from the example of a similar experience.

"Brenda, I remember how I reacted when my mother died. I know it's not the same thing you've gone through—and I understand that many counselors have said that to be divorced is the most difficult adjustment a person may have to go through—but there is a part of my experience that might transfer over, and that is this: I found it very valuable to talk with others about my sorrow, my fears, the good and bad times we'd had together. That talking was very healing, and because it was, it was easy to overdo it without realizing it. I had to learn to take it easy on my friends. To not wear them out with the same thing over and over."

The self-disclosure was appropriate and offered Brenda valuable advice. It confronted with the truth gently, but was easy for Brenda to ignore the message. She did.

A gentle confrontation seeks to nudge the person, in contrast to tying them up and running away with them. This minimizes risk and resistance and makes it easier to give.

Gentle confrontations must have enough intensity for the message to be thoughtfully heard, yet can be brushed aside for the time being.

Gentle confrontations may talk about people in general rather than a specific person, use "loophole words," may include humor, and include quite a bit of affirmation. The nonverbal style is assertive. The tone of voice carries both concern and caring. Eye contact is regular. Body posture and gestures are relaxed and assured.

The confrontation is expressed tentatively, allowing for the possibility that things may not really be the way they seem to be. It is expressed as opinion, rather than fact, because opinion can be cast aside more easily.

A gentle confrontation seeks to help the person confront self. A confrontation from self comes from inside the walls of defense. Therefore, it has to be noticed. There is virtually no risk to creating an atmosphere in which the other person can confront self. This is done by helping the person review the facts systematically, so that the discrepancies are laid out side by side so the person can easily notice them.

Moderately intense confrontations. Joyce reported how the complaining affected her. "I'm feeling sort of uncomfortable myself now because I think I see a pattern—especially during the last month or so—of repetitive complaining about particular things. It's kind of a turn-off."

Brenda said, "Oh, I'm sorry. I don't want to do that."

She meant it. The friendship she felt with Joyce was very important to her. Sure, there had been a few times when she had thought Joyce didn't care about her, but she saw in Joyce an unselfish concern that other people didn't have.

Brenda knew that Joyce would not give up trying to help her. She didn't like what she heard but she liked Joyce, so she thought about what she had said.

This is the "I-message" pattern, often taught in assertiveness classes. It simply *reports* to the other person the effect their behavior has on the person reporting. It is more intense than self-disclosure because it deals with the behavior of the other person.

Last week Joyce said, "Brenda, you seem to be putting a great deal of your thinking and your emotional energy into the things that are wrong. You've told me about those things and, believe me, it looks like things are through right now. But you have a lot of persistence and creativity in you. It's always shown up in your teaching. You don't seem to be using those gifts—the persistence and creativity—to help yourself with these tough circumstances. I think you need to."

And Brenda replied, "Oh, I think I'm doing everything I can possibly do to help myself."

As she heard herself say it she knew she didn't believe

that. But it's tough for any of us to admit we've been living below our level of competence. She felt affirmed by Joyce and recognized the truth, but she was not yet ready to act on it. This confrontation points out Brenda's failure to use her personal strengths for her own benefit. It is affirming, but also very direct.

A tough confrontation. As an example of a tough, effective confrontation we will use the confrontation Joyce gave Brenda early in this chapter.

Joyce had done a lot of listening and she understood as best she could what was going on in Brenda's life. She tried gentle confrontations but these hadn't helped. She had made some mistakes, especially the outburst of the harsh confrontation, but she had cleared these up with Brenda and the two of them had developed strong mutual caring and trust. All of this prepared the way for this latest conversation.

The ultimate effectiveness of a confrontation depends not so much upon what happens at the moment of confrontation but upon the love and trust that have preceded it. We try to avoid rudeness and misunderstanding, but if we keep pursuing what is best for the other person the effective things we do will outnumber the ineffective and our blunders will not destroy our relationship.

Tough confrontations are deliberately more intense. Affirmation of the other person continues but now the spotlight is on the specifics of the discrepancy. Intensity increases when the confrontation is personal and specific. We are not talking about discrepancies in people in general but about a particular thing at a particular time in the life of the confronted person. We deal with actions rather than words, more intense because it is harder to explain away behavior than it is to explain away words. The nonverbal style is assertive, carrying more concern and urgency, perhaps at the expense of warmth, than in the gentle confrontation. We are persistent, relentlessly bringing the person back to the discrepancy. We ask for a plan, using such questions as: What do you think? Do you agree? What are you going to do about it? How will you do it? When?

It is most intense when we use the other person's system to contradict what he or she is doing now. We work within their system of thought and behavior, using data and authority from sources they trust. For example, if they say they accept the Bible as their guide for living yet persist in malicious talk about others, we ask them about Colossians 3:8 which condemns that behavior. Now it becomes confrontation from the Bible— confrontation from within their own belief system—instead of confrontation from you. This is harder for them to ignore.

A game plan. In general, the idea is to begin with gentle confrontation and, if necessary, to increase the intensity until the message gets through.

When to confront? When the message is accurate and the other person is ready to receive it. How do we know that? The accuracy comes through preparation of listening and discernment that is guided by the Holy Spirit. The timing will also be guided by the prompting of the Holy Spirit.

One should still check inner impressions against guidelines such as:

• We confront to protect a person from his or her own actions, or to protect others.

• Confront when the person is showing motivation to progress in life. Perhaps they are confronting themselves about other matters, increasing self-discipline, persisting toward improvement in other areas of life.

• Confront when other methods of helping a person progress in life are not working. You listen and support and develop trust and have shared yourself with them through your disclosures but they still need direction and push from the outside in order to move.

• Confront when they are "nibbling at the edges" of confronting themselves but they won't do it. They are hinting that they need confrontation but cannot do it entirely on their own.

• Do not confront when: it would hurt the other person more than it would benefit (to point out discrepancies they cannot do anything about); to show off; when you have a "holier-than-thou" attitude; just because someone else wants you to confront that person; or when the risk is too great.

The last we knew about Joyce and Brenda, Brenda had fled from the room with apparent anger and Joyce was trudging home feeling sad and guilty. As may happen, the effect of a successful confrontation may not be known for some time. In this case, to find out what happened you only need to read the next chapter.

Discussion Questions

1. Define *confrontation*. Give your opinion of the author's statement," Confrontation is a powerful force for better or worse."
2. Relate an instance in your life when confrontation turned out to be a good force in a relationship.
3. How is confrontation an act of Christian obedience?
4. What is the most important part of our preparation for confrontation with a person?
5. Upon what factor does the success or failure of confrontation usually depend?
6. Discuss the various styles of confrontation and relate an incident from your own experience to illustrate.
7. Evaluate Joyce's attempts at confrontation with Brenda.
8. When is it best not to confront?

Chapter Eleven

Taking Responsibility: Apologies

Brenda felt resentment surge within her. She looked at the 20 persons seated around the circle and felt 20 different kinds of resentment, or perhaps 40 or 60.

Fellowship group, she thought with disgust. *They should call it the Look-Down-on-Brenda group!*

She knew she was filled with bitterness and she knew that the way out had to begin with her willingness to be responsible to do all she could for herself. She resented the group for teaching her that and hated herself for not doing it, but resentment still gave a little cheap satisfaction and her woeful accounts of the divorce still eked out a few moments of attention.

She sat with arms crossed, her hands clutching her arms. Her knees pressed tightly together and her feet pushed on the floor; her legs ached with stress. She wondered if this would be the night she would lose control and tell them all where to go. She half hoped so.

Dear God, she prayed silently, *what's becoming of me? I'm losing control of my job, I can't stand my friends, I can't sleep—I'm being murdered by my own anger. God, why don't you let me die and get out of my misery!*

Her eyes darted from person to person, fearful that

they knew her thoughts. She returned a smile with a grin that was too wide and too rigid to fool anyone and her stomach tightened with contempt for her own phoniness.

The pastor said, cheerily, "Isn't it good to be together again! It's Thanksgiving season, and I'm thankful for this group! You people mean so much to me!"

Brenda's mental critique of the pastor began. *You call us "people" like we're the troops out here to follow your commands. All I mean to you is a number in the Sunday morning head count, dollars in the plate, a face in this Wednesday evening fellowship farce!*

Brenda's fingers dug deeply into her arm, jolting her out of her angry thoughts. The group was singing: "They will know we are Christians by our love, by our love."

Her stomach knotted like a clenched fist. She wanted to scream out, "Sure—love, love, love. But it's all love for yourselves! Nobody here loves me! You're all too busy talking about how much love you have to use any of it! I will know you are phony by your indifference."

She pinched her eyes shut, tighter, tighter, as if to snuff out the spark of life within them and then, through tears, glared at the pastor who was singing ". . . by our love, by our love . . ." She thought, *If you could only see my disgust for you and this whole frumpy group it would knock you off your chair!* The thought amused her.

Her thoughts churned on, thoughts honed razor sharp by repetition. It had been 11 months since Jack had phoned to say divorce papers were on the way, that he'd come over when she wasn't home to get his clothes and would she please leave the extra key to his car on the kitchen table. In her mind she paged through the months of disbelief, denial, hope, despair, self-doubt, and confusion—one painful memory after another. She felt the anger at Jack, but much more intensely the recent anger at the church and the pastor, those from whom she had wanted acceptance, encouragement and guidance.

Drenched in the storm of her memories, Brenda was only dimly aware of the group. The pastor was saying ". . . so that's what I'm thankful for. What are you thankful for?" He looked around the circle.

Joyce spoke promptly with a concise list, Roy added something about copious harvests, and Grace mentioned her new granddaughter. Brenda jumped back to reality when she realized the reports were coming around the circle.

I can't fake it, she thought as Fred spoke from six chairs away. Her mind scurried to find something trivial and safe amid the chaos of her thoughts. Five turns away, four, three.

Her thoughts alternated between jumping to her feet to run away and jumping to her feet to shout her anger at the group. Two people away. One. She felt numb. Her turn.

She took a deep breath. Mouth closed, she wiggled her tongue, trying to get a sensible response started. "Well, uh, of course I agree with everything that's been said so far. As for me, uh, it's been a pretty tough year you know. You know that, of course. We've talked about that. A lot, really. Well, there's something I'm thankful for— yeah, I am. A lot of you have done a lot of listening. I guess you really have. You didn't have to, but . . ."

Brenda stopped, mouth poised for words that didn't come. She was surprised by sudden understanding of something that Joyce had said yesterday, "Brenda, you're not going to get over this thing until you decide that you don't have a right to insist that other people listen to you."

That was when she had walked away from the conversation, but now she knew that Joyce's statement was true. She had coaxed and pushed and whined and intruded, and had been resentful when others had given only the amount of time they could and not the amount she wanted. She now saw that she had acted like a parasite ready to bleed the emotional energy out of others, only to demand more and then sulk and complain when it wasn't offered.

The group fidgeted in the silence, knowing that Brenda had more to say. She sensed the eyes on her, felt hot from shame, and ached over the nuisance she had been to others.

She fumbled for a beginning. "A lot of you have listened. Uh, thank you for that. Yes, thank you." She glanced around the group and back to the floor. "I guess I've been pretty rude and not any fun to be around. I'm sorry. Oh, it's been a lot worse than that. Worse than you know. You don't know what resentment I've felt. All the nit-picking and stupid little grudges I've had in my heart toward each of you. Some more than others."

The room, tense with uncertainty, was shattered by Brenda's shout. "Oh, what's the use of trying to say it right? I hate you people and I love you! I hate myself and I want to love myself! God forgive me for the hate—it's not what I want. I want us to all love each other. I see I've not been doing my part. I've had it all backward.

"I've wanted your love but I've tried to force you all to give that to me. Okay, you're supposed to, but it's not my job to enforce that. My job is to give to you, and I haven't given a thing!"

She paused to think, then went on quietly. "I have a lot to be thankful for—a good job, health, two invitations for Thanksgiving dinner, the clear blue sky and sunshine this afternoon, family members even if they live a long way from here, and this group. I can't believe I say that because I have found fault a million times in my mind with you, but it's true that you have been friends.

"Especially you, Joyce," shaking her head in disbelief at her words, "especially yesterday when you told me straight out that it is I who need to change, not them. You were being my friend when you said that. Now I see what you meant. Forgive me please, each of you, for being such a pain in the neck, for not appreciating how much you have given to me, for demanding instead of giving. I love you. Forgive me."

It was quiet. Everyone was thinking, searching for words to accept Brenda's apology, but no one felt qualified. One person leaned forward to speak, then pulled back. Grace opened her mouth and lifted her hand, only to slowly murmur, "Oh, never mind."

Roy spoke first, saying, "Pastor, there's something I want to say to you, but privately. Is it wrong to ask if I can do that now?" As they stepped outside the room, Ann, followed by three other women, darted over to hug Brenda.

A description of what went on next probably should not be attempted. There were a lot of quiet apologies and affirmations, a lot of tears, a lot of hugging. The only really important element was the Holy Spirit helping people find words, courage, and humility. Apologies and forgiving dissolved the pain of suspicion, competitiveness and bitterness; peace and love flowed in. Evidence of relational healing was seen in the softening of facial lines, glistening of eyes, unselfish listening. Everyone knew it.

Late in the evening as the group stood in a small circle it was Brenda who started the song, "They will know we are Christians by our love . . ."

Brenda cried in bed that night. That was routine, but these tears were of gratitude and hope, not pity. She also took inventory, which was another routine, but tonight she counted blessings and aspirations, not grudges.

Tonight she had apologized to the group. She knew it was the beginning of a new way of thinking and acting— that her apology was her promise to not repeat the behavior that was offensive to others.

She knew she had been forgiven. She had heard persons forgive each other. And she had forgiven them. If all that had been possible, it proved that she could forgive Jack, didn't it? She was sure it did. She breathed a prayer of thanksgiving for that assurance.

Just before she fell asleep she smiled, soft and sincere. It was the beginning of a new routine.

That's the way it happened, unexpected and explosive. It was a typical apology in only one way—it was born of pain—but it included the essential elements. Within herself she had confessed and repented before God, and received His forgiveness. She told the group how she felt, took responsibility for her sins against them, and pledged that her future behavior with them would be based on love.

The Elements of Apology

An apology is an act of strength. It is evidence of maturity that you already have and it helps build greater personal maturity. The important part of an apology is not what you say, but what you mean. The words of your apology tell another person about your feelings, attitudes, and intentions, but it is how you live that out that counts.

To apologize is to say that you are sorry:

Soon
Offer
Regret and
Restitution
Yourself.

We will consider these one by one.

Soon. The earlier you do it the better. That is difficult, because it means a commitment to change the direction of your attitudes or change your behavior. But putting it off is difficult too. Our minds begin to imagine the other person laughing at us or accusing us or talking about us. It doesn't pay to wait.

We may procrastinate in the hope that we will forget about it. Sin doesn't let us forget. We try to cover our guilt with layer after layer of excuses and frivolity, or maybe even good works, but there is no silencing the effects of sin without repentance and, when possible, apology and restitution.

Offer. An apology that is pulled out of you is only hollow words—nothing. The worth of an apology comes from the intention to change future behavior and it can be only you who controls that. If you don't intend to change you're not really sorry, and if you're not, don't say so, for that only adds phoniness which is also wrong.

Regret. This means that you wish you hadn't and that you won't in the future. The evidence of your regret is your covenant to make your future behavior better than past behavior.

Restitution. This is to do the best you can to compensate for the damage you've done, to seek to restore the situation back to the original condition. Sometimes you know exactly whom to go to and what to do. John was in the middle of a 450-mile trip when, in the middle of the night, he had a flat tire. He put on his decrepit spare tire and drove carefully into the next town. He found a car with good tires on a dark street and stole a tire. It was so good he thought, "Why be wasteful?" and took another. Five months later he went back, found the owner, and paid. Hard? No doubt! Risky? Certainly! Worth it? John says, "Absolutely!"

Other times it can't be done with that precision. Paul found a wallet at church. Careful to not look for a name in it, he took the money from it and left it where it was. Several years later this action bothered him. The real owner could have been identified at the time of the wrong-doing; now he couldn't. Paul felt release from his sin after sending an extra contribution to the church.

It is possible to go too far with this and to develop an unhealthy concern about restitution. That is an outgrowth of what is often referred to as neurotic guilt or false guilt, and may be an indication of seeking God's pleasure through works rather than accepting His grace.

Everyone has done things about which they might feel guilty. If we chose to, most of us could spend full time trying to track down and clean up every sin-bred mistake we make. We'd never get caught up, we'd seem weird to others, and we'd be neglecting other important parts of our spiritual and personal responsibilities.

Protection against excess comes by checking the four points of the Christian's compass: (1) God's Word; (2) His truth as revealed through reliable sermons and other teaching; (3) communication with God through prayer and the guidance of the Holy Spirit; and (4) counsel with mature brother and sister believers. Take frequent compass readings to keep yourself on track in this bewildering area as well as others.

Yourself. You made the mess, so you clean it up. There is no other way.

How to Apologize

It is easy to learn the right words. Describe the incident you are apologizing for as simply as possible, and just say "I'm sorry." Such as: "I spoke unkindly yesterday morning. I'm sorry." Or, "When I laughed at you a little while ago, it was inconsiderate. I wish I hadn't." Or, "I should have talked directly with you about it instead of talking with our neighbor. I apologize."

Speak your words of apology simply and specifically, short so that neither of you is unduly embarrassed. Avoid a holier-than-thou tone. It will often enough be painful to apologize, but it is humble obedience, not pain, that makes apologizing an exercise in spiritual growth. As for the pain, it will probably be greater as you seek to put your resolve into better behavior.

It's easy to know how, but not easy to do. That is why we should ask God for His help. Sometimes we get annoyed with God for expecting us to apologize, and then don't ask Him to help us do it. God wants relationships between persons to be restored through processes such as apologizing and forgiving; He will always help us.

It is worth the effort to apologize. It helps the other person, but your benefit is even greater. It frees you from guilt and shame about your own behavior and, usually, from their retaliation or from your fear of the retaliation. Basically, though, we do it in obedience to God's wishes for us.

How to Benefit from Being Confronted

We need to make sure that we understand the confrontation accurately. That means listening well and then checking along the way to make sure. You might ask the other person to repeat to you what he has said or, even better, restate what you have heard so he can check it for accuracy.

Avoid the self-pity trap. If you get your car stuck in the snow don't spin the wheels; that just makes it sink in deeper. Wallowing in self-pity is similar. Receive the confrontation and then start doing the hard work that is involved in order to move forward.

Try to avoid defensive reactions—to argue, to not listen, or to try to explain away what they are saying. Avoid retaliation. When we are confronted, often the first thing we want to do is to go talk to someone else and start criticizing the person who has criticized us. Or another technique more subtle and even more effective is to wait for the person who has criticized you to blunder. Make sure he knows that you know about it. You might even make a point of being obvious about not criticizing him or you can say to someone else, "You wouldn't believe what this person did to me." Fighting dirty, isn't it? Dastardly. But so human! Do you do it too?

Ask yourself, "Am I willing to bear the cross of criticism

for the sake of Christ?" If we can see criticism in its larger perspective as a means toward more complete personhood and more effective service to Christ, perhaps we can be less defensive.

Jesus bore the cross of criticism. He behaved just as Isaiah 53:7 foretold He would, "Oppressed and afflicted, yet He did not open his mouth."

Don't brag about the amount of criticism you get. If your life is so limited that criticism is the only thing you have to revel in, you're missing out on the better blessings.

Still, valid confrontations can be painful and it is proper to share that pain with a trusted friend. Do that in a way that does not give an unnecessary burden to the person you are talking with. You might best leave out names, for example. This is especially important when the criticism was invalid or given in an unjustifiable way.

Ask yourself, "Am I doing my best with what God has given me?" In the midst of criticism which may be hampering your performance in one area of life, are you still doing the best you can in the other areas?

Ask yourself, "Is the criticism valid?" If it is, it's all the more painful and you need it. Don't write it off immediately—take a close and prayerful look at it. Take the words at face value. Let the other person say what he feels, but for his sake and for your own do not let him be abusive.

Don't get overinvolved in trying to interpret why he is saying what he is saying. That's his business; you concentrate on learning what you can from the content of what he is saying.

Ask yourself, "Am I guilty of criticizing others?" People criticize us and we get bent out of shape and go right about criticizing others. Each of us is prone to get upset about our own weaknesses when we see them in other people.

Ask yourself, "Am I asking God to confront me?" There are things that God teaches us in our times of silence before Him when we are willing to bear the cross of criticism. God's confrontation is always accurate, always at the right time, and always in our best interests. Ask yourself, "Am I thankful for this confrontation?"

If a person confronts you with constructive purposes, it is usually an indication of deep caring for you. It is hard to remember that at the moment; in fact, the first thing that pops into your mind is probably that he doesn't like you. It is a beautiful thing when we have persons in our lives who love us enough to confront us about destructive or negative attitudes or behavior.

Cleaning up the messes we've made is a necessary first step in gaining release from conflict with others. When we learn from confrontations to us, and take responsibility for our offenses to others through appropriate apologies and restitution, then we can move on to forgive others. With that, God can heal the wounds that others have inflicted on us. Forgiving, as we shall see in the next chapter, opens the way to confident joy and freedom in relationships with other persons and leads to more complete understanding of God's love for us.

Discussion Questions

1. Identify the major reason for Brenda's resentment.
2. How do you account for the change that came over Brenda as she began to talk about "being thankful"?
3. Do you agree with Joyce's statement that Brenda doesn't have a right "to insist that other people listen to you"? Or do you think that as a part of the Christian community she does have a right to insist on their listening to her?
4. What effect did Brenda's asking forgiveness of the group have on the individual members of the group?
5. Why is it so important to apologize soon rather than procrastinate? What are your experiences with this?
6. What is your feeling on asking God to confront you? Share a personal experience about that.

Chapter Twelve

Freeing from Resentment: How to Forgive

She said, in words as brutal as broken glass, "I'll never forgive you in a thousand years!"

He said, "If you think I'm going to forgive *you* for what *you've* done, you're out of your head! This is the first day of lifelong contempt for you, if I think of you at all, which I won't."

Forgiving is difficult—perhaps the act most contrary to our human nature, which prefers revenge to unselfish love. We don't want to forgive so we contrive excuses.

Her best friend said, "Don't give an inch. Let him hang himself with his own rope. It will teach him a lesson."

His best friend said, "That was too big and too rotten to overlook. She doesn't deserve to be forgiven."

Forgiving means giving up all claim upon one who has hurt you. It includes letting go of the emotional consequences of the hurt.

God demands that we forgive because the failure to forgive is hurtful to us for two reasons: (1) we begin judging and dispensing punishment, activities which God reserves for Himself; (2) we become knotted with resentment which saps our emotional strength, chokes our relationships with others, and limits our freedom to live joyously.

The following story about forgiving is told as it happened:

"It was one of the most important events in my spiritual development, also the scariest thing that had ever happened in my life.

"I hadn't been a believer in Christ very long but I was firmly convinced from the things I had seen and heard that Jesus Christ was the Son of God. Those were exciting days as we saw the power of Christ at work in people's lives and as we looked forward to the fulfillment of His promises.

"They were also troubled times, however, especially for believers. My country had a long history of violence and there were reports that believers in other places not far away were being persecuted—men and women dragged out of their houses and thrown in jail. At least one had been killed.

"Opposition was strongest in the capital city. One man, the kind of manic, crazy man who draws attention and controversy everywhere he goes, opposed us on religious grounds of his own, and he had a lot of support. I hadn't seen him and I hoped I never would, for I despised him. He persecuted our brothers and sisters in other places and caused us to be afraid. We kept a low profile because we heard his opposition was spreading.

"We knew Christ taught about loving your enemy and we wanted to follow His teachings. My friends and I concluded that the best way to do that was to worship Christ and develop spiritually so when the time came to be of service we would be strong. In the meantime, it just didn't make sense to take chances.

"It had always been exciting to hear how God worked dramatically through people but I wasn't about to volunteer to have a miracle worked through me. Little did I know. Before bedtime one night I thanked the Lord for peace in our city, for the comforts of home, and I asked for a quiet night of sleep. I didn't get it.

"The Lord spoke to me. I couldn't believe it at first. I thought maybe I was crazy. I tried to talk Him out of what He was asking me to do. The task was this: the man—our enemy—was in our city and I was to go where he was staying and give him a message from the Lord. My choice was between obedience with fear and possible death or disobedience with guilt. I would rather have been crazy than face that choice.

"It was just daylight when I went. The last of the night people were stumbling home and the morning people were purposefully about their business. I was afraid, but determined to be obedient.

"I went there and rapped on the door. Three men answered. They were afraid of me, not knowing that I was even more frightened. They frisked me for weapons before they let me in; yet I had the impression they expected me. They led me in to see the man. He was in bed.

"I stood there and, in quaking voice, blurted out the message, 'Brother Saul, the Lord—Jesus, who appeared to you on the road as you were coming here—has sent me so that you may see again and be filled with the Holy Spirit. Receive your sight.' Just like that he began blinking and something like scales fell from his eyes.

"I went on with the message the Lord had sent: 'The God of our fathers has chosen you to know His will and to see the Righteous One and to hear words from His mouth. You will be His witness to all men to what you have seen and heard. And now what are you waiting for? Get up, be baptized and call on His name.'

"He got right out of bed, slowly because he had had nothing to eat or drink for three days, but it was easy to see that he was a man of energy and action. I, an ordinary believer named Ananias, baptized him.

"He stayed awhile with us in Damascus. It was really great to learn from him because he understood how God's truth was fulfilled in Christ's life, death, and resurrection. He taught us that not only did belief in Christ give us eternal life—good enough—but better than that it gives us power to change life here on earth. He was an ideal example of firm belief and fearless behavior.

"He told me once much later that he admired the trust in the Lord and courage I had shown in visiting him. He said the Lord had told him to wait for instructions that would come, but that he couldn't imagine until it happened that the message would come through one of the believers whom he had come to persecute.

"Saul was confronted by God: he confessed, repented, and was forgiven by God. Also we forgave Saul for his sins against us and he forgave us for our animosity, fear, and mistrust.

"It was tough at first to trust Saul. He had a reputation you couldn't ignore and there was nothing subtle about the way he acted, even after he believed. His logic had finesse, but his personal style was blazing. We learned to know him, then trust him, and then to love him.

"The local leaders plotted to kill him and we had to smuggle him out of the city in a basket. As it turned out, that clandestine retreat was the opening scene for his life of service to the rest of the world.

"Those of us in Damascus had already learned some lessons that would be valuable all our lives. We learned that the Lord's work was served by forgiving. We learned that the Lord is dependable. The experience has been useful to me lots of times since then as the Lord has asked me to do hard things. None of them has been as dramatic as the encounter with Saul, but every time I have been obedient to the Lord it has proved to be good for me and has proved that we have a loving Lord. I wouldn't trade that fact for *anything.*"

Forgiving is something each of us must do frequently, yet it rarely comes easily and never comes naturally. For you to forgive is . . .

—*an impossibility* because it is so contrary to your human nature which cries out for vengeance against the person who hurt you. But, even though impossible for your human nature to attempt, it is at the same time

—*a necessity,* because if you do not forgive you will be forced to live in a cage of resentment—a cage that will grow smaller and smaller until it crushes you and resentment rots away all joy and meaning from your life.

Forgiving is—

—*an open choice.* You have as much choice over whether or not you forgive as you have over anything, yet for the Christian it is also

—*a command.* Christ says, "But if you do not forgive men their sins, your Father will not forgive your sins" (Matt. 6:15).

Forgiving is—

—*a precious treasure* that cannot be bought at any price by those who seek to receive it, yet it is

—*cost-free* to those who wish to give it away.

Forgiving is—

—*unavailable.* The powerful cannot receive being forgiven by force; the eloquent cannot coax it by persuasion; the wise cannot derive it through logic; and the clever cannot synthesize it in the laboratory. It cannot be gotten at all—forgiving can only be given. Yet the glorious gift of forgiving another person is

—*freely available.* It is one of the inexhaustible resources that can be given just for the wanting to. It is available for the giving in plenteous measure to young and old, rich and poor, the famous and the unknown.

Forgiving is—

—*complicated;* for while the debate between "forgive" and "don't forgive" swirls back and forth across your mind you can think of nine thousand reasons to not forgive. Yet you want to. It is bewildering. Fortunately, forgiving is—

—*simple.* All you have to do to do it is do it.

Forgiving is—

—*detested* when it is up to us to give it, but

—*desired* when we wish to receive it.

Forgiving is—

—*a gift from you to me,* to release me from my guilt, present or future, because of what I have done—or haven't done—that hurts our relationship. But equally it is

—*a gift to yourself.* When you forgive me you are free to be shaped by God into His pattern for you, to move toward the wholeness of person and fullness in living that He wants for you.

Forgiving is all of these things, but best of all forgiving is—

—*an opportunity* to experience the Lord working in complete partnership in your life—the Lord soothing your angry heart, molding your thoughts, giving you words and the courage to say them, teaching you love, and it marks

—*a new beginning* because when you forgive, God expands your capacity to feel clean and free and at peace, and He packs that capacity to overflowing with His love. Then you can move ahead in life with greater strength, with greater confidence, and with new understanding, based on your personal experience of the reality of God's unlimited love.

Why We Need to Forgive

Forgiving is commanded. "And when you stand praying," Jesus said, "if you hold anything against anyone, forgive him, so that your Father in heaven may forgive you your sins" (Mark 11:25). The theme of forgiving appears in Paul's letters in terms clearly not optional: ". . . forgiving each other, just as in Christ God forgave you" (Eph. 4:32) and "Forgive whatever grievances you may have against one another. Forgive as the Lord forgave you" (Col. 3:13).

We should not "keep score" on forgiving, thinking that our forgiveness of others is a prerequisite to being forgiven or that God's forgiveness to us is in proportion to how much or how perfectly we forgive others. But the message is clear: forgive.

God wants us to forgive others so we will be aware of our own sins and ask for His unlimited grace. As we fail to forgive others we remain blind to our own sins, stubbornly persist in continuing to sin, and do not ask for God's forgiveness. It is when we most clearly see the destructiveness of sin in our relationship with other persons that we see the destructiveness of sin in our relationship with God.

There are no greater opposites than our sins and God's holiness. The ultimate example of forgiving is His forgiving our sins. He asks us to forgive those who have sinned against us, a task similar to His own but a pinpoint in size compared to His mercy.

Not forgiving destroys relationships with others while forgiving teaches about relationships. We need relationships with others to be whole and joyful persons. Forgiving is a growth experience and helps build a platform for more growth.

We need to forgive for self-preservation. Not forgiving prolongs hurt and anger and leads to long-term smoldering resentment which will make us miserable until it kills us. Resentment destroys the perception of reality. As we begin trying to bend the world to accommodate our resentments, fear, and selfishness, we begin to be less accurate in understanding the world. This begins to destroy our ability to cope successfully with life.

We forgive for the sake of the forgiven person, that he may be released from a sense of guilt. And, in forgiving we are an example to others. We lead them toward renewal through Christ.

Why We Don't Want to Forgive

We are sinful by nature. Sin is selfish, forgiving is unselfish. Our pride seeks revenge even at the cost of self-destruction rather than unselfish love.

Forgiving is considered weakness within much of American culture. This is a misunderstanding of what strength is and an acceptance, if not adulation, of violence and revenge.

There are some false benefits of not forgiving. It may feel good to hurt—a neurotic satisfaction from licking our wounds. Vengeance can be fun for the attacker, *briefly.* It is easier to not forgive. We may get others to feel sorry for us because we have been abused by others. Any satisfaction that comes from these sources is just the sugar coating on a pellet of poison.

We are afraid to forgive. It may leave us open to being hurt again. If we act in a mature way this time we may have to live up to it in the future. When the person we need to forgive is the only other person in our life with whom we have a strong emotional tie, even though it may be an unpleasant one, we may fear being more lonely by losing that relationship. We may fear that we do not know how to go about forgiving. In some cases, we may be so accustomed to feeling bad that we are afraid to discover that we can feel good, either because that would be unfamiliar or because that might not last.

We may not want to forgive because we are guilty in our own behavior and are reluctant to apologize. Or we may hurt so badly from what has happened that we are still emotionally unable to forgive.

These are often more than just excuses—they are tough obstacles to overcome. Begin anyway—confident that God never asks us to do the impossible—and proceed step by step.

Signs of Needing to Forgive

Use this as a personal checklist. Any of these can be related to other matters, but if you see any of these signs in yourself think carefully about any way in which you have been hurt but have not forgiven the person who hurt you:

□ Do you feel hurt, wounded, put-down, humiliated by another?

□ Do you think often about a hurt? This is the seedbed for resentment.

□ Do you think about difficulty or injury coming to a particular person who hurt you?

□ Do you avoid communication with the other person when communication is appropriate? Do you avoid the person?

□ Do you suffer physical symptoms: tension, tightness, stomach disorders, insomnia?

□ Is it easy for you to get angry about other things? When resentment piles up from one source is it easier for you to overflow with anger coming from other sources?

□ Do you indirectly attack the other person? For example: do you spread stories, try to turn other persons against him or her, or keep that person from benefits he or she should have?

□ Do you directly attack the other person? For example:

physical attack, insults or sarcasm, withholding money, jealousy tricks.

□ Are you highly critical of self?

Steps in the Process of Forgiving

God teaches us how to forgive. We have scriptural principles to guide us. We have the prompting of the Holy Spirit. And we have examples of forgiving: Esau to Jacob, Genesis 33:4,11; Joseph to his brothers, Genesis 37:5-36 and 50:19-21; Moses to the Israelites, Numbers 12:1-13; Jesus to His enemies, Luke 23:34; and Ananias and other believers to Saul.

Do you *want* to forgive? Probably not.

Are you willing to forgive? I hope so, for it is only then that you discover that forgiving brings far more than it costs.

Forgiving is a process that begins with a conscious decision at a point in time. It moves from that willful mental decision to resolution of the fears, resentments, and vengeful urges against the one who has hurt us, and from that to behavioral expressions of love toward the person. This process faces the formidable resistance of our human nature which does not want to forgive.

Sometimes the process is completed in a few minutes, as we saw in the previous chapter; but often it is eked out through inch-by-inch yielding of our selfishness. How quickly it happens depends on how willing we are. It happens only with God's power combatting sin, power available to us through prayer. We shall describe a sequence through which the process often goes.

Forgiving begins with a deliberate decision. The decision may be to forgive, or to be *willing* to, or to *become* willing to. It matters not so much where we start as that we start, and that we move along as best we can. We begin honestly where we can, do what we can, and God's grace makes up the difference. For many persons the beginning would include the following kind of petition:

A Prayer of Willingness to Learn to Forgive

Heavenly Father, you ask me to forgive others. It seems so hard, and I've tried so often and failed. When I consider your forgiveness to me, whatever forgiving I might be able to do seems so paltry and incomplete. I can't do it on my own.

Help me learn what I need to know about how to forgive. Help me discover the wrongs that have been done me for which I need to forgive others. Grant me wisdom and courage to be obedient to missions of forgiving. Teach me how to allow the love that you have for me to flow through me to others, so that relationships are restored and your will is done.

In forgiving, as throughout all of life, we should have ongoing dialogue with God through prayer. In this we should thank God for His forgiveness to us, ask God to reveal to us the sins we commit and how they affect others, and confess and repent as we learn more about ourselves. Without prayer, the following suggestions are unlikely to accomplish much.

This list is a guide—suggestions to help you get started with a specific project in forgiving. The items are listed in the order in which they often occur but there is a lot of individual variation. Not all of these items apply every time. Not all of them will be necessary, or even possible, in a given situation. The process will go better if you pray about it first. Remember, forgiving is not something you earn, but something God does to you and through you.

1. Quit hurting the other person. Forgiving is the opposite of vengeance—you can't do both. If you have really chosen to forgive, you will quit doing the things that are contrary to forgiving.

2. Decide that you are willing to want to apologize and forgive. You begin where you can begin; for many people this is the first step. You're not forgiving, you don't even want to now, but you believe that you should and you decide that you are willing to begin wanting to.

A Prayer of Commitment to Forgiving

Heavenly Father, forgiveness is something you have freely given me. I don't understand it, or why you have forgiven me, but I thank you for it. You want me to forgive others. It seems so hard, because it seems so unfair that I should forgive when I have been mistreated. Yet I will, with your help. Right now I commit myself to forgive those who have sinned against me. Teach me how. Give me the courage to do what you help me see that I should do and to proceed with your wisdom and love flowing through me. Amen.

3. Begin to want to apologize and forgive.

4. Determine if you should talk to the other person about your forgiving them. See guidelines about this later in this chapter.

5. Make amends for your part—apology and restitution. See chapter 11.

6. Forgive.

7. Claim the forgiving and forgiveness—the closing of this incident. Offer a prayer of thanksgiving for the closure.

8. Pray for healing of the memories. Memories are not

erased from the brain—we can forgive but we probably can't forget. But the damaging effect of the memories can be neutralized. God is not controlled by what has happened in the past and He wants you to be free from being controlled by the past. Pray for freedom from guilty feelings, fear, alienation, or whatever has been associated with the incident you have forgiven.

9. Now that it's closed, keep it closed. Refuse to think about it any more.

Should I Talk to the Person I'm Forgiving?

Sometimes you should talk. You have a right to report to other persons that they have hurt you. You have a responsibility to report wrongs against you by other Christians so they do not continue to sin (see Luke 17:3).

Sometimes you shouldn't talk. Again from Luke 17:3,4 we see that we do not forgive verbally unless the other person repents. Any time you give this kind of report it is likely to make the other person uncomfortable in some way—perhaps embarrassed, angry, or ashamed. It may bruise his ego. You should not talk if it would damage him more than it would benefit him.

Be very cautious when the hurt is immense, the other person's ego is weak or the other person in some other way lacks emotional flexibility, and/or there is no way for the damage to be compensated for. This latter situation is common in regard to hurt inflicted unintentionally by parents.

Sometimes you can't talk. The other person may be dead now, he may absolutely refuse your invitation to dialogue, or he may be physically remote. Or, while we may be able to meet face-to-face, the other person would simply not be emotionally or mentally participating in the conversation either because he is not motivated or because he has lost the capacity to be involved.

We always are to forgive in our hearts. As a general rule we should always take the initiative to apologize for our sins; rebuke the other person when appropriate; but wait for him to repent before talking with him about forgiving him.

How to Talk with Other Persons About Forgiving Them

Determine if you really should talk with the other person. Prayer is essential, and talking with a trusted Christian friend can be very valuable in this decision.

Rehearse the conversation of forgiving. There are three benefits from this: (1) you practice doing what you are going to do; (2) as you practice you learn a lot about yourself, your behavior, and about the other person; and (3) your attitudes may begin to change.

One method of rehearsal is to imagine that you are forgiving the other person. Picture it and hear it in your mind the way you want it to happen, with the conversation coming out the way you would like it to. Look ahead to success.

Another method is to talk with a friend. Ask someone who understands your circumstances, who cares about you and has the emotional energy to invest in helping you, to play the part of the other person. Say what you would like to say to the other person.

Tell the other person that you want to talk, face-to-face if you can. Don't make a big production out of setting this up. When you do talk, make it easy for the other person. Keep your anger out of it because that will probably only raise defensiveness. Remind yourself that your forgiving is only possible by God working through you.

Apologize. See chapter 11 for more information.

Listen, no matter what. Listen for cues to whether you are exaggerating or diminishing your ideas of what has happened. Listen for greater insight into your sins against the person. Listen to communicate your acceptance of him—acceptance which you must have in spite of not accepting his behavior.

Report how his behavior has affected you. You may state that both of you are responsible for what has happened but do not state proportions and do not be overly apologetic.

Make a statement of forgiving. If it is proper for you to talk with him about it at all, then make a straight out "I forgive you." It doesn't have to be those exact words but they're hard to beat for being quick and easy to understand. They may be hard for the other person to believe, but that's not your problem. Explain why you want to tell him this.

Affirm the other person as a person. Give the message, "You as a person are worthwhile." If you can't say that with no strings attached, you haven't yet forgiven him in your heart.

Forgiving Multiple Offenses

Forgiving does not change the other person or protect you from more hurt. I often am painfully reminded of that in my counseling office.

The first time I talked with the young woman her knuckle-white hands clenched the chair arm, fingers pinching deep into the upholstery. Her entire body was rigid with rage—so tense as to seem brittle, yet vibrating with restless hostility. All that energy was compressed into the cutting edge of her voice as if it were a fishhook slowly ripping open her husband's face. "I can forgive him for hitting me when he was drunk, but I'll never forgive him for running all over town with that floozy and everybody knowing about it but me!"

Well, her reaction to what had happened is so typical

of us all—willing to forgive in part, but not completely. That's the way we react, quite in contrast to God's encompassing mercy.

Okay, so we are human. That just means that forgiving doesn't happen all at once; it is usually a process over time, not completed in one mighty "zap."

But neither should we look at it as something we eke out on our own. We can't. We are responsible for doing what we are capable of, step-by-step. Often, when we take the first difficult, painful, faltering step, God gives us the capacity to move quickly through the remaining steps. Sometimes it's difficult all the way through. Either way we learn through adverse experience and discover how God works with us to accomplish what we cannot do alone.

The thing that is important is that you begin where you can begin. Forgive what you can forgive. Then pray for willingness to forgive the rest. As you can, forgive those matters. But don't be surprised if you remember more offenses; deal with these one-by-one.

When there have been many offenses there may be only one occasion in which the forgiver talks with the other person, and maybe not even one. Even if there could be more, it often is not advisable or necessary.

It is important that you continue to remember that the essential element of forgiveness is your heart attitude, not the words said to the other person, important as those may be.

Living the Forgiving

You do often remain involved in the life of the person you have forgiven. Again there is no set formula—you may be with him a lot or it may be only an invisible, emotional tie—but you seek appropriate ways to express God's grace and mercy to him. You may:

• Affirm him, support him, in your words or actions.

We read in Proverbs 25:21,22, and quoted by Paul in Romans 12:20, "If your enemy is hungry, give him food to eat; if he is thirsty, give him water to drink. In doing this, you will heap burning coals on his head, and the Lord will reward you."

- Pray for him.
- Leave him alone if he finds your presence abrasive.
- Witness to God's mercy in your own life.

In summary, you are one of God's representatives to him. That's always a heavy task. Don't do it alone, because you don't have to. Pray for wisdom and patience. It's a joyous task when we are obedient. Pray with thanksgiving for God's healing in your own life and for His presence within you.

> Lord, the miracle of forgiving has happened. You have forgiven me and you are teaching me to forgive others. Help me celebrate these miracles and to recognize always that it is only with your love that the tyranny of pride and resentment can be broken. Let there be no condescension— no looking down my nose at the person I've forgiven. Instead, give me opportunity to be of service to that person whether through my deeds, my words, or my silence. Keep me vigilant to my opportunities to serve and to my tendency to again be vindictive and petty. Thank you again for your loving forgiveness to me made possible through the sacrifice of Jesus, in whose name I pray. Amen.

The story of Ananias is a good example of putting devotion into practice as Peter urges in 1 Peter 4:7-11. We don't know much about Ananias; before God worked in his life he may have been as unlovely as Saul. We know that he loved God enough to listen to Him and be obedient to Him. It was that love that made it possible for him to overcome the fear that he must have had in going to visit Saul.

What might God have in store for us? The way we find out is by obedience, even if it calls for the growing pains called "forgiving." Whatever it is, obedient forgiving leads to glorious consequences our minds are too small to dream of.

Discussion Questions

1. What are some reasons for the fact that forgiving another person is so difficult?
2. Describe Ananias's dilemma in the task of obedience to God.
3. Why is it imperative that Christians forgive? What Scripture can you give to substantiate your answer?
4. How is forgiving "a gift to yourself"?
5. What is meant by "keeping score" on forgiving?
6. What are some "false benefits" of not forgiving?
7. How do you feel about forgiving a person who has mistreated you when that person has not asked you to forgive the wrong?
8. What does "living the forgiving" mean to you?
9. Who do you need to forgive?

Chapter Thirteen

"Commission Me, Lord"

It's normal to have problems and conflicts. If it isn't normal, why do you and I have so many? So did Christ. So did Paul. It is the result of sin in the world, so we can expect it. But we can rejoice with Paul through it all knowing that none of the afflictions can separate us from Christ and that in Christ we are victorious over death. (See John 15:18-25; Rom. 5:3; 8:35; 12:12; 1 Pet. 4:13.)

But that's the long view—what about the here and now? Again, victory. We are overcomers in this life because God helps us.

He helps us directly and through other persons—our servant friends. If they serve us and we serve others, our tiny hunk of the world begins to be a better place.

That works, as this example shows: Several years ago I was facing a major vocational challenge—a lecture that was quite important to me. I was looking forward to it and had prepared rather well, but about four days before I was to make the trip I was suddenly drenched with anxiety and the feeling of incompetence, almost to the point of thinking I couldn't carry out the presentation.

I called my friend Gary Sweeten who traveled from another city to be with me. For two days we talked and prayed; he taught and the Lord showed me some areas in which I needed to forgive. The Lord helped me do that. There was dramatic release from some very old inner turmoil, a surge of confidence, and the lecture engagement went uncommonly well.

From that experience I learned some things about God's healing processes. I taught those things to a young woman, whom I shall call Shelley, a patient assigned to me in the hospital's outpatient department. When she used these principles in her own life the Lord freed her suddenly from the effects of an old trauma in her life and helped her move on very quickly to a new level of personal effectiveness and spiritual devotion.

Shelley gave me permission to share her story with others. I told the story in a workshop on forgiving. A lady whom we will call Elaine heard Shelley's story and recognized those circumstances as being similar to her own.

Elaine wanted what had happened to Shelley to happen in her life and came in for counseling. Over a period of several months there was remarkable change in Elaine's life. She began to care about others and gained a new level of confidence, personally and within her family.

Her father had been active in his church all his life but had never known peace and joy in his own heart. He had abused Elaine verbally and physically for many years in her childhood. Gradually, as Elaine's attitude toward him changed, there began to be changes in his attitudes. For the first time ever, he hugged Elaine. It was on her thirty-fifth birthday. Praise the Lord for family renewal, no matter when it happens!

At this point it had been two years since Shelley had

been in. I phoned her to see how things were going. Now, rather than staying away from work because she was afraid, as she had frequently done, she was the person her supervisors held up as an example to other workers and the one they all sought out for their own strengthening and encouragement. Praise the Lord for organizational renewal!

There is a man in Elaine's neighborhood who used to be known as the neighborhood grouch. The younger children were afraid of him, the older children hassled him, and the adults avoided him. One day Elaine wandered over to his yard and struck up a conversation with him as he was working in his garden. They pulled weeds together and she listened to his grumbling longer than she wanted to, until she had a chance to share with him some things that had happened in her own life. She taught him some things about forgiving.

He used what he learned; he changed. Even the people who weren't looking for it noticed it. They could hardly believe it but they liked it. He did too. Praise the Lord for personal renewal!

Servant friendship. Gary had responded sacrificially to my cry for help. Things he taught me were shared with Shelley, made a difference in her life and helped her become able to help others. Her story was shared publicly and had an effect on Elaine. Elaine passed the good news on to her father and to her unfriendliest neighbor.

Servant friendship—doing what you can to improve the lives of those around you, reinvesting the help you receive, relating to others on the basis of their best interests.

It works. Shelley helped Elaine, whom she has never met, not because she set out to but because she was obedient to do what was set before her. She has helped many others in the course of being a loving person. Elaine helped her neighbor, not because she wanted to but because she was obedient to do what she saw needed to be done.

Servant friendship. Powerful because it is God's power flowing through the life of an obedient believer. Thank you, Gary, for being my servant friend. Thank you, Shelley and Elaine, for living out the Lord's principles unselfishly and courageously.

Thank you, Lord, for your perfect, unfailing love, the ultimate friendship. Thank you for the truth of your Word, for fellowship with my brothers and sisters, for the promise of peace eternal.

Teach me the things I need to learn to be more like you, as a servant friend to those around me. Help me keep Christ as the direction of my life. Help me recognize opportunities of service and to have the patience, unselfishness and courage to do what I know to do and the faith to venture with the Holy Spirit into expressions of grace that are new to me.

Commission me, Lord, to be a servant friend whenever, wherever, one of your creatures can use a touch of your love through my life.

May I remember that every good thing that happens is of your hand, and praise you in every thought, word, and deed. Amen.